Law and Society
Recent Scholarship

Edited by Melvin I. Urofsky

A Series from LFB Scholarly

The Real ID Act
Privacy and Government Surveillance

William Eyre

LFB Scholarly Publishing LLC
El Paso 2011

Library of Congress Cataloging-in-Publication Data

Eyre, William, 1960-
 The Real ID Act : privacy and government surveillance / William
Eyre.
   p. cm. -- (Law & society : recent scholarship)
 Includes bibliographical references and index.
 ISBN 978-1-59332-456-8 (hardcover : alk. paper)
 1. Identification cards--Law and legislation--United States. 2.
Terrorism--Prevention--Law and legislation--United States. 3. Privacy,
Right of--United States. 4. United States. Real ID Act of 2005. I.
Title. II. Series.

 KF4791.E97 2011
 342.7308'58--dc22

                                              2010052923

ISBN 978-1-59332-456-8

Printed on acid-free 250-year-life paper.

Manufactured in the United States of America.

To my son Richard, who is growing up and must live in the society we are creating. And to my parents.

CONTENTS

vii

ACKNOWLEDGEMENTS

Thanks to Dr. Eugene Spafford at Purdue University, whose Center for Education and Research in Information Assurance and Security interdisciplinary program is an example that others should follow. Thanks to Dr. Victor Raskin, Dr. Josh Boyd, Dr. Aaron Hoffman and Dr. Christian Hempelmann, for their help and guidance.

I'd also like to thank all those who have helped me along the way and Carol Bowser for helping to prepare the manuscript.

INTRODUCTION

American society is struggling with the issue of surveillance and the loss of individuals' privacy. Surveillance and the technologies used, and implications for the future of American society are examined in this volume.

Public Law 109-13 contains the Real ID Act, and the implementation of this act and others like it has far-reaching ramifications for Americans' privacy. The Real ID Act, an example of recent laws regarding privacy and surveillance, serves as a basis for discussing the development of the surveillance society and its effect on American citizens.

The new surveillance system erodes personal privacy and creates a threat to privacy and autonomy from both criminals, the government, and due to insider abuse of data, criminal members of the government. There is a possibility that Real ID information access can be used against people in ways both legal and illegal. Whether the government is capable of responsibly handling increased amounts of information regarding its citizens is in question. Such resources appear to only provide opportunities for improper gathering of and access to and misuse of personal data.

For most people, the developing surveillance state may only pose a potential danger. However, when someone is identified as a target, the potentially devastating effect of government scrutiny threatens participatory democracy and the expression of legitimate political dissent.

The discussion of these issues in this book can increase awareness of the erosion of privacy rights which, once surrendered, become increasingly difficult to regain. Additionally, there are questions as to the validity of the security assumptions that are used to justify the erosion of constitutional protections.

CHAPTER 1.

Surveillance Today

A Day in the Life

It's an average day. Winston and Julia Smith live in a high-rise condominium in Chicago and start the day by tuning to the morning news. Their television is fed using a cable box, TiVo or satellite connection and the couple watches the program on a High Definition Television (HDTV). The television signal provider logs and stores the information regarding the channels to which the Smiths tune at any given time, down to the second, and allows the provider the ability to record in a computer log file those preferences. Additionally, if the individual has a Digital Video Recorder, the time and duration, as well as the content of the show being viewed, are also known to TiVo or whatever company administers the DVR software updates and management. (Charny, 2004)

DVRs conduct two-way communication with the entertainment content provider, gathering information on users' viewing choices, ostensibly for the purpose of giving entertainment consumers other, similar or related viewing choices. In order for this goal of predicting users' preferences to be achieved, the shows the consumers watch must be known to the preference prediction algorithm on a computer. This algorithm determines recommendations to the users based on that user's past viewing. This recommendation scheme also rests on some assumptions. Mainly that the targeted individual watches and enjoys the shows that appear on his/her screen. In cases in which the consumer leaves the power to the television on when out of the room or house, or uses the television to entertain guests, the assumptions start to break down

However, in its most basic form, the "recommendations for future viewing" feature is implemented using an algorithm which determines the genre and subject matter of shows the users appear to like. At the algorithm's heart is the "rational choice" model in which it is assumed that users will only view the shows they like and not select and view

1

shows they do not like (such as if they were assigned to watch a show for school or an influential person in the targeted consumer's sphere asked the consumer to watch a certain show.) The algorithm then fits the users' past selections to a set of preference scoring criteria, picking other shows and/or movies matching those scoring criteria and recommending the resultant list to the viewer. This process is analogous to the manner in which Amazon makes recommendations to its customers regarding books the targeted consumer might prefer ("Million Dollar Netflix," 2006).

This information has commercial value and is stored indefinitely. It also has value in that it can give insight into individuals' interests. This viewing information provides data for content programmers and the types of organizations possessing the requisite motive and resources for understanding the psychology of the viewer.

Additionally and in a similar fashion, the HDTV itself uses a bi-directional data transmission protocol for the digital data that comprises the pictures, sound and metadata that comprise a transmission. The two-way communication feature of HDTV was written into the specification in order that consumers could conduct video teleconferences (Svensson, 2008).

If Winston or Julia were to connect a personal computer to the HDTV itself, with the HDTV acting as the monitor (screen) for the computer, the Smiths could perform all of their computer functions they would normally perform using the HDTV display. The Smiths could also connect their Webcam in this configuration and the HDTV would provide higher definition fidelity when communicating with people at the other end of an Internet connection for a chat session. The generally unintended consequence of communicating according to the parameters described in this scenario involves the fact that everything displayed on the HDTV acting as the computer monitor may be transmitted as data to the other end of an HDTV connection as a separate data stream of which the Smiths are unaware. This data stream would be in addition to the data communication with the other end of the Internet connection. The communications would be transmitted easily as two separate connections. These connections could be to two essentially dissimilar places, as the processor in the HDTV (the computer that converts HD digital signal to build the picture) by definition has enough processing power to render the picture itself into a digital signal. This signal could then itself be sent to wherever it is told.

In the very near future, the Smiths will not need a Webcam in order to transmit the goings on in the field of view of their television. Apple holds a patent which describes a television screen with sensors interlaced amongst the pixels which compose the display portion of the TV. These sensors interpret the photonic input they receive to allow the TV itself to act as a camera. To zoom and pull out, the array selects smaller or larger subsets of sensors which provide variable focal lengths. This serves the purpose of the TV having the capability to transmit close-ups and wide angle views (Fox, 2006).

One or both of the Smiths might then sign onto the Internet and check email. If one of the Smiths visits a government Web site, under a recent United States Department of Homeland Security (DHS) Cyber-Initiative, established by classified presidential order, any communication that traverses a federal government network may be recorded by the National Security Agency (NSA) or DHS (Nakashima, 2008a). The reason given for recording visits by American citizens seeking information from government Web sites is in order that the United States is protected from terrorist cyber-attacks. All visits to government sites (i.e., IRS, CDC, DoJ, etc.) are recorded and NSA monitors and records all communications including Internet, voice and email (Bamford, 2008). AT&T also monitors the contents of Internet communications in real time (Singel, 2007) and could easily record all the traffic that crosses their backbone.

In addition to any monitoring and recording of Web use and email traffic by the government and the backbone provider, all visited Web addresses and emails are recorded in the ISP's database. Each click on an ad or link proffers a new piece of information for the ISP's database. The addresses of Web sites visited as well as the content of those sites are also, in the default configuration of the most used Web browsers, stored on the user's hard disk. The reason for this storage is that the browser will then speed up the display of data (text and graphics) from the "cache." ("Deleting Web Browser", 2006) It also leaves a permanent, barring user intervention, record of everything the user had "seen." (Certain assumptions are necessary; that the user did not click on a link which maliciously redirected them to a site not described by the link, and that those links which were clicked correctly offered sites and pages that the user then actually viewed.)

In the Smiths' high rise condo's hallway there is a camera. When they leave their condo, their images are recorded by a camera in the hallway. When they have visitors, the visitors are photographed entering and leaving the Smiths' condo. The elevator has camera. As well the elevator lobby, main lobby by the guard's station and doors to the outside are under video surveillance, as is the parking garage and the garage's entrance.

Winston works in the suburbs and drives to work from the city. Julia works in the city's center ('the Loop' in Chicago's case) and takes mass transit.

Some transit systems have migrated away from paper tickets which can be paid with cash to "Smart Cards" ("About smart cards," 2009). In some cases, transit systems have variable charges based on a trip's length, such as in Washington, D.C ("SmarTrip Questions," n.d.).. In Chicago, the trips are fixed price but the principles are the same ("Information about Chicago Card," n.d.).

For the transit system to charge the correct fare, the customer's entrance and exit points from the system must be known. When a transit customer boards a train at a certain platform, the customer uses the Smart Card and the location and time is transmitted to and recorded in the database. Smart Cards communicate through the distributed Smart Card sensor network (i.e. the entrances and exits to the transit platforms at which the contactless cards are presented.)

The system processes the information on the entry and is performed in order to automatically deduct the amount of the travel from an account (card.) The account must be filled with money and this can be accomplished using a credit card. The ostensible purpose of the Smart Cards is to save money for the transit system and eliminate the fraud involved with people passing transfers to each other in order to get free rides (Godfrey, 2008).

Once the credit card is used for the purpose of payment, the transit card number and the credit card number are linked. Log entries must be made and kept of all transactions at each stage("SmarTrip Questions," n.d.), and therefore all the data associated with an individual's transit system travels are known forever and can be mined or viewed any time thereafter ("Intelligent Transportation Systems," 2005).

Data mining is the technique of using databases as input for algorithms that search for patterns and identify characteristics and generators of patterns in which the data analysts' end users are interested ("Data Mining with MicroStrategy," n.d.).

In Winston's case, that of a commuter driving to work, the fact that he owns a car is registered with his state's motor vehicle bureau. The fact that the vehicle is registered can, on its own, be considered a minor issue in terms of surveillance. Vehicle registration has been required for many years for purposes of taxation. Massachusetts was the first state to issue registration tags in the United States in 1903 (Tortora, 1998) and these tags are basically tax receipts and therefore the tags show credit for the proper vehicle registrant. For surveillance purposes, the vehicle's plate number can be associated with an individual owner. If Winston stops for gas and pays with a credit card, the transaction is logged into multiple databases (O'Harrow, 1998).

There are now Radio Frequency Identification (RFID) readers along highways. The Transportation Recall Enhancement, Accountability and Documentation (TREAD) Act rules mandate RFID chips to be embedded in tires. Uniquely numbered RFID tags in individual tires tie the tires to specific vehicles ("Intermec to support," 2002). The stated goal of the Act is to facilitate recall efforts in the case of recalls of defective tires by matching each tire to the vehicle and by extension, the owner. As Winston drives to work, he may encounter one or more of these RFID readers, and the time and location of the encounter is then be logged into a database (Warrior, McHenry, & McGee, 2003).

The other technology that can be used to track vehicles is the Tire Pressure Monitoring System (TPMS). TPMS is a technology mandated by the National Highway Traffic Safety Administration and was be implemented in all new passenger cars and trucks starting in 2007. The stated *raison d'etre* of the sensor is to detect whether or not tires are under-inflated (J. Kerr, 2007). The sensor transmits a unique ID number to the on-board system, mostly on one of two assigned radio frequencies, 315MHz or 433MHz. These signals can be picked up at a distance with a directional antenna, and the initial ID number assignments are made by the auto manufacturer. These ID numbers are recorded in the database(s) in which all of the other part numbers associated with that car are recorded. Some sensors are embedded in the wheel assembly, and the tire must be removed to access them. These devices have batteries which last 7 to 10 years. Another option is to use a valve stem sensor as the TPMS beacon (D. Kerr, 2007).

All supported cell phones have, at a minimum, location assisting technology, and newer cell phones have assisted-GPS. The assisted-GPS cannot be turned off and will work even if the Subscriber Identity Module (SIM) card is taken out of the phone or switched with some other phone's SIM card (K.C. Jones, 2007a). (The SIM card contains the numeric codes which link the phone to the subscriber.)

The SIM card also contains a subset of the phone book data and text messages, including deleted text messages. This information can be recovered forensically, so the system can even know exactly where the user was when having sent any given message ("Sim card," n.d.). As Winston is driving along, because of the two way communication that defines a cell phone, his location is logged by the cell phone company, possibly as often as every couple of seconds if the parameters are set that way at the cell provider's data center. This type of location and tracking mechanism is in place ostensibly in order that if Winston becomes lost or missing, the cell phone tracking records can be used to reconstruct his movements, and then to find him ("Missing Persons," 2008).

Many new cars have on-board computers which record information. Some of this information regards the condition of the engine and various on-board systems. These on-board computers also maintain continuous records of the car's speed at any given time. There are 30 data points that the federal government is going to require of all electronic data recorder (EDR) equipped cars. The EDR will be a requirement for all new cars sold starting in the 2013 model year. As of 2008, many manufacturers have started equipping their cars with EDRs. In most cases the EDRs write over old information as new information is recorded. The overwrite time is variable, but specified so that the 30 data points are available for a time long enough that in the event of a crash, the insurance company and law enforcement can determine what the car was doing just prior to a crash.

In some cars, a vehicle status data recorder, which does not overwrite data and is always-on, is included. The ostensible reason for installing this device is for manufacturers to determine if and when a driver violates the warranty, and what part (or parts) is (are) affected by the behavior which would void the warranty, such as racing (Gritzinger, 2008).

The onboard Global Positioning System (GPS) device communicates using a digital signal allowing the car's location to be precisely fixed at any given moment. This is a two-way communication which causes real time location information to be written to a database, and this information can be stored, or referenced through a tracking database. Various commercially available products facilitate the storage and retrieval of GPS-generated location data, and they are used for various purposes. Police and intelligence agencies use GPS tracking on suspects' vehicles, with and without warrants (Hubbard, 2008). Likewise, car dealers who sell vehicles to customers who the dealer feels may one day need to have their car repossessed sometimes have GPS tracking devices on the vehicles and do not tell their customers about this "feature" (Vijayan, 2008). Some systems have components associated with the GPS that can be controlled from a PC. For instance, the person controlling the system, in addition to knowing where the car is at any time, could disable the starter ("GPS Vehicle Tracking Systems," 2008).

Winston may need to pass through a toll booth to get to work. Several tollway systems offer toll transponders which have the toll amounts automatically taken from an account which is charged with a credit card. Each transponder is uniquely numbered so that the correct amount can be debited to the correct account for toll payment. The time and ID number of the transponder are written to a database for billing and to settle disputes. More recently the toll records have been used, not just for criminal investigations, but also in civil cases such as divorces, to prove the car was not where the lying spouse said it was at whatever time was in question (Newmarker, 2007).

The same toll lanes which offer this convenience also have cameras. The cameras photograph the vehicles that pass through the transponder lanes, and the reason given for having the cameras is to prevent fraud and misuse, and of course send tickets to those without transponders ("E-Z Pass," 2006). The fraud could consist of such instances as someone manufacturing a counterfeit toll transponder programmed with someone else's correctly guessed or deduced transponder ID number, or something as simple as the use of a stolen transponder. (Of course if the owner notices and reports the theft, the toll passing capabilities would presumably be shut off at the central computer.) Transponders can also just be hacked, with the bad guy able to read another individual's legitimate transponder and then use the transponder code (Mills, 2008).

Winston will still have his travel recorded by a camera. Many toll booths are dual use and can take cash and still read the toll transponders. The cameras are trained on cars traveling through in those lanes ostensibly to combat fraud and abuse and for crime prevention in general. Cameras for tracking cars via license plates are used in law enforcement's patrol cars.

The leading manufacturer of license plate readers (LPR) is Remington-Elsag. The Mobile Plate Hunter 900 system consists of cameras mounted on a squad car. The cameras read the target vehicle's plates use optical character recognition (OCR) software to identify the characters of the plate and use a connection to a database to check the plates for various violations. The system can read up to 900 plates per minute from up to 50 feet with 95 percent accuracy (Vlahos, 2008). Checking the plates once they are read is a trivial computer database lookup problem.

The government in Britain started testing a new camera in Britain in 2010 that can read cars' plates, check for currency of vehicle tags, measure speed for speeding tickets, measure the distance between cars to detect tailgating and enforce seatbelt laws by taking pictures of the individuals in their cars (Morris, 2010). Presumably, some similar system would become available for local governments in the United States shortly after this testing period is complete.

When Winston arrives at a garage in an urban area, the car is photographed on entering the garage, and Winston pushes the button for a ticket which contains a magnetic stripe. When Winston exits the garage, if payment is made with a credit card, his identity is associated with the garage ticket (which contained the entry time and by inference a cross-reference to the pictorial record of entry) and the car's visit to and length of stay at the garage is written to a database. The stated reason given for this type of observation involves physical security (Haas & Giovis, 2008).

If Winston parked on a city street in a downtown urban area and received a ticket for staying in the space for longer than amount of time than for which he paid the parking meter, that information is entered into a database ("Parking Ticket Management Solutions," 2008). There had been a surveillance effect of police department parking patrol personnel patrolling the streets with handheld computer-like wireless devices, but that was the old way. Today, the fact is that many cities have instituted laws which require that cars which have more than a certain number of outstanding tickets logged against them to be booted, i.e., fitted with the "Denver boot." Parking patrol in Chicago canvasses the streets using 26 vans, each equipped with LPRs and checking cars on both sides of the street at 1,000 cars per hour. The license plates of the cars are compared to a list of wanted license plates (Washburn, 2007). The most efficient mechanism involves transmitting the license plate of the parked car to a central database and having the computer make the database lookup from the centralized database. There is nothing to prevent the time, location of the query from being logged in the database, and many reasons to expect that the recording of the encounter will take place. Even if Winston's car is parked legally, if a parking patrol van drives by, the city or whatever agency is interested will know when and where his car was parked.

Many convenience stores, malls, commercial buildings and public thoroughfares now have digital video surveillance cameras trained on the pedestrians and patrons. The nine-inch black cube hanging behind the Starbucks team member's head is a security camera (O'Harrow, 2005). So when Winston goes in before work to buy a cup of Starbucks, his image is recorded, and presumably, if he pays cash, his preference can still be deduced using the record from the digital video camera.

If Winston or Julia withdrew cash from an Automated Teller Machine (ATM) on their morning break, the time and location, and picture from the ATM camera is duly stored in a database ("Digital Recording," 2004). The ostensible purpose of this type of surveillance is crime and fraud prevention and detection.

At lunchtime, Winston may buy something for his wife with a credit card, maybe for her birthday, maybe a purse she admired. That credit card transaction, including a detailed list of items purchased, is recorded. There is likely a camera recording the transaction, and at any time in the future, that transaction's video can be accessed keyed on the financial transaction itself (Vlahos, 2008). There may be cameras in the lobby and/or trained on the building entrance at work. Those cameras will record his return to work. As of January, 2008, there were an estimated 30 million surveillance cameras in the United States recording the goings on in public and publicly accessible commercial spaces. These cameras were recording 4 billion hours of images per week (Vlahos, 2008).

When Winston swipes his card for access to restricted buildings and areas, that information is recorded in a database. Winston uses a computer to do his job. Many employers have installed monitoring software to ascertain what exactly Winston, and other employees like him, do on their computers. At the very least, the bandwidth providers know what he does on the Internet. Some corporations and government agencies employ key loggers, which record every key the computer user strikes. So when Winston sends his wife an e-card for her birthday, the boss will know. Of course many employees avoid doing any personal business on the computers at work for the reason that they are monitored. The reason given by employers for using key loggers and other monitoring software is to measure employee productivity and monitor activity, perhaps to prevent the theft of insider secrets or other nefarious actions on the part of the employee ("Internet and Computer," n.d.). This type of surveillance, however, is expected, as employers merely state in the employee handbook or wherever their policies are published that the employee has no reasonable expectation of privacy when using work-related resources (Eureste, 2008).

Every phone call is logged to the telecom's databases, and recently, legal authority to conduct real-time wiretapping against wide swaths of the citizenry has been granted by the United States government to itself (Frederickson, 2008). This authority is in addition to the warrantless and illegal wiretapping which occurred starting in 2003 and in some limited form even prior to that, in 2001 and before (Bamford, 2008).

The scope of the illegal surveillance and the number of calls illegally wiretapped will never be known. The FISA Amendment Act gave the telecoms retroactive immunity for illegal actions committed by the telecoms which were in violation of the FISA law as it had stood at the time the crimes were committed. Mark Klein, the AT&T employee who came forward with evidence of the criminality offered to testify to Congress about the crimes he witnessed. He was never called to testify by any committee of Congress. His lawyer's letters offering the testimony were never answered. He eventually said, "There will never be any hearings. It will die, and you'll never find out what they did." (Goodman & Klein, 2008)

The supposed reason for wiretapping Americans and storing the phone numbers citizens dialed, citizens who were under no reasonable suspicion and for which the government certainly had no probable cause, was that this type of Fourth Amendment violation was necessary for anti-terrorism purposes. So Winston Smith calls his accountant, and the phone number he calls is entered into the database. Quite possibly his conversation was recorded. It is well within the capabilities of the NSA to digitize and record every phone conversation made by every citizen.

Winston Smith may call his banker, or broker, or travel agent, or his host at the casino. Because all of these individuals work at commercial entities which are classified as financial institutions under the terms of the PATRIOT Act II, his records, along with everyone else's who has dealt with these institutions, can be seized by the federal government without a warrant (Wolf, 2007). He could easily be made the target of wiretapping (Risen & Lichtblau, 2005). No one will ever know if his conversations are listened to by some agency of the government, because the names and details of eavesdropping targets are classified.

In many large commercial buildings in urban areas, those entering must present a driver's license and sign a book in the lobby. There is nothing to prevent the names in those visitor logs from being entered into some type of database. Some would say the security types would be remiss if they did not enter the information into a database. The accepted reason for this type of information gathering is that the guards must physically secure the building and somehow this information helps them to do so.

Most public and commercial spaces in large cities are under video surveillance. In urban areas, intersections in high-crime areas and intersections deemed to have a high rate of accidents are under video surveillance. Cameras are used to issue traffic citations by mail for red light violations (Washburn, 2007). The camera feeds are sent to centralized "command centers" in which human operators may be watching in real time. In heavily surveilled cities, such as Singapore or London, individuals in the city centers may be photographed as often as 300 times per day (Murphy, 2007). The reason given for taking everyone's pictures all the time is to prevent crime, investigate crime, and for traffic safety. Currently, there are plans to install more video surveillance cameras in urban areas in the United States for anti-crime purposes ("Big bucks," 2008).

When Winston leaves work, the surveillance regimen marches on: cameras record his walk to the garage, the garage card reader system logs his exit, the toll transponder and camera log his travel down the expressway, the RFID readers silently read his tires' RFID tags, the GPS and cell phone tracking systems mark his minute by minute progress, the computer in his car records every acceleration, every deceleration, every stop, every go. When Winston gets back to his high-rise in the city, more of the same – until finally the last thing at which he looks before going to sleep, the least email he reads, the last Web page he views for that day, is recorded.

On the weekend, every book Winston checks out of a library is recorded. Sometimes, however, the government has trouble collecting that information legally (Kronholz, 2003, Reutty, 2007).

Every airline ticket anyone purchases and every rental car agreement into which anyone entered results in database entries, recorded forever. Every time Winston writes a paper check, when it is processed at the bank, a computer scans the image of the check and that picture is stored in various databases. If the check is to the "wrong" person or for too much money, these determinations being made by the government, the Federal Government is informed through a separate channel and program (*Bank Secrecy Act*, 2006).

Any time Julia signs up for a loyalty card (the cards which allow discounts on selected items when presented upon checking out at supermarkets and other stores), the company issuing the card will want to the person's name and address, phone number, and age. The reason given by the merchant has to do with marketing. Many want the option to mail sale papers to the loyalty card holder. Mostly, however, the marketers are building a dossier (marketing profile) on the individual.

When Julia shops, a record of all of her purchased items is stored in a database such that even if she pays cash for the purchases, every item purchased is associated with Julia ("Loyalty & Stored," 2004).

If Julia (or Winston) gambles at casinos, the casino loyalty cards, when used in machines in a casino, are used as the key in the machine or at the table to create exact records of all of their gambling activity. In the case of the slot or video gambling machines, these records are precise in time to the exact second and in amount to the penny of wager and payout. In some casinos, the machines are networked and this information is available in real time to casino management. The casinos maintain that this type of surveillance is useful in order that if an individual is losing, the casino can offer that patron some type of perk. With the free meal, or whatever incentive the casino dispenses, the gambler feels better about losing their money and will return more readily to play again (Binkley, 2004).

If Winston trades in the stock market, Security and Exchange Commission (SEC) records what stocks people buy and when they buy those stocks and then the agency stores all of the information regarding every transaction. The ostensible purpose is to detect activity which would indicate insider trading activity (Countryman, 2003).

If Winston and Julia travel to an international destination, they are outside the sphere of American surveillance, and subject to the surveillance apparatus of the country to which they travel. Some countries, such as Britain and China, have as much or more in the way of a surveillance apparatus as the United States (Hope, 2008, Klein, 2008). Most countries have less. For United States citizens, the government has a very comprehensive surveillance system in place. The system has been developed to track the identities of citizens entering and leaving the United States. Key tools in this surveillance include passports and Enhanced Drivers Licenses (EDLs) ("Overview of Enhanced," n.d.) to conform to the Western Hemisphere Travel Initiative (WHTI) ("WHTI," n.d.).

The WHTI was authorized by the Intelligence Reform and Terrorism Prevention Act of 2004 (IRTPA) and went into effect on June 1, 2009, and "requires U.S. and Canadian travelers to present a passport or other document that denotes identity and citizenship when entering the U.S." ("WHTI," n.d.) Aside from a passport, EDLs are acceptable travel documents for U.S. citizens to use to re-enter their country. The EDLs are RFID chipped driver's licenses which also have a machine readable zone - optical character read (MRZ-OCR). As of October, 2010, four states and four Canadian provinces are issuing EDLs. These are Michigan, New York, Vermont, Washington, British Columbia, Manitoba, Ontario and Quebec ("Overview," n.d.).

The repository that the U.S. Government uses to store the data is the "Border Crossing Information" (BCI) system ("FR Doc E8-17123," 2008). U.S. citizens' border crossing activities are entered into the BCI and the information will be held for 15 years. Americans have some say as to whether and how they are tracked at the border. According to Bonnie L. Rutledge, Vermont's commissioner of motor vehicles, "A person opts to go over the border, their information is going to be collected and held anyway. If you don't want to go over the border, you don't have to." (Nakashima, 2008b, para. 22)

Data Fusion and Integration

All facets of surveillance involve gathering and managing data. Organizations recording transactions and location data include significant amounts of ancillary information associated with each transaction and geo-location data point. For instance, a retail chain, when storing information about a cash purchase at a store conducted using a loyalty card, include or link to data elements such as the individual's phone number, email address and postal address, which should not be strictly necessary for logging the transaction. These additional data fields are required by at least one grocery store chain in the Washington, D.C. metropolitan area when a user wishes to sign up for a card online. This chain has a multi-state presence. Ostensibly, the marketers are interested in the demographic data for building dossiers.

Acxiom is one company that aggregates all manner of publicly available information to build dossiers (O'Harrow, 2005). The extra information makes data fusion easier.

Data fusion is the key to linking databases together to link and make accessible the maximum amount of data regarding each individual being tracked. Data fusion is an important concept for data mining and data integration in surveillance applications. Data fusion, in its most basic sense, involves matching sets of data to each other based on common data elements in the data sets. The additional data attached to those common elements are then added to the dossier (Garfinkel, 2008).

In the case of recent voter roll purging incidents, registrars and officials claimed non matches in the data on the basis of as little as a single character being different between the subject's name as it was input and the name listed in the voter database (Goodman & Weiser, 2006). The criteria for data matching were very strict as the purpose of these voter roll purges is to remove voters from the rolls. In contrast, when tracking and tracing individuals, it is desirable to integrate data points, so the rules allow for more leeway regarding the possibility that two similar names are associated with the same person, and the algorithms more able to match data to various individuals. The purpose of data integration is to chart connections between elements of information in such a way as to easily track information associated with an individual, even in cases of incomplete or inaccurate informational elements.

Integration is the act of connecting data about similar subjects from various sources (Rao & Tripati, 2008). The data may have characteristics with varying degrees of similarity. The similarity could be that the data fields match up character for character (as in the example with the voter rolls above,) or the data fields could be dissimilar. When the keys, or main identifying fields, such as names or Social Security Numbers (SSNs), of the data are identical in each of the databases being integrated, the job of integration is easy. Most of the types of information available to a logically centralized database have various inconsistencies, misspellings, different forms of a name, similar names and different addresses for the same individual, etc. With information integration, when a misspelling is encountered, other information can be compared, allowing for an identity match or association of an informational element in percentage certain percentage of cases. The process by which this type of information matching is conducted involves resolution or reconciliation of the data (Bhattacharya & Getoor, 2007).

An example of integration might be the following: Winston is carrying Julia's cell phone because his cell phone broke. He might have to borrow a friend's (let's call him Aldous) car. Thus, when Winston is driving along, the RFID readers (from the tires and toll tags) and the geo-location data from OnStar (Biggs, 2001) indicate that it is Aldous driving along. But the cell phone geo-location tracking data show that it is Julia. Then Winston parks in his regular parking garage and swipes into work with his ID. There is now a higher percentage chance that it is Winston because it is unlikely the car or cell phone owner will swipe into Winston's office during business hours. At this point, the integrated system can then correct the location tracking database to indicate the correct individual's movements (Winston's.)

The integrated system will also note that Julia is somewhere else because her transit card was used on the transit system, in accordance with her patterns, and Aldous' first car (he loaned Winston his second car) and Aldous' cell phone are seen moving along Aldous' normal route at the correct time. So even though the informational data points taken individually (cell phone, car) might have led to a mistake in tracking Winston, the integrated system can make the correct identification. This is the type of situation that becomes a selling point for VeriChip, the company that has received FDA approval for its RFID chip to be implanted in humans. VeriChip claims 100% accuracy of identification of the correct human when the system is functioning normally (Greene, 2004).

In the late summer of 2008, the National Reconnaissance Office (NRO), which is responsible for conducting surveillance using earth-orbiting satellites, started working with DHS to aim the satellites at American territory and American citizens. The program is known as the National Applications Office (NAO). Previously, privacy, national security considerations and other limits on the federal government's powers to conduct surveillance on American citizens prevented the use of military satellites to conduct surveillance of the United States and

American citizens. The ostensible reason for the satellites looking down on America and Americans is to find weak points in security defenses and to conduct other "anti-terror" operations. A recently released Government Accountability Office (GAO) report noted that the program "lacks assurance that NAO operations will comply with applicable laws and privacy and civil liberties standards." (Gorman, 2008) The program is moving ahead nonetheless.

Beyond the details of tracking and surveillance of movement in public spaces, there are aspects to tracking and surveillance at a wider level of integration. This integration involves commercially and publicly held data.

Acxiom is one of a number of companies that aggregates and integrates public and transaction records. Aggregation starts with the procurement of large databases with information from one or more sources. The databases are then integrated with existent information in new, proprietary databases, or set up as standalone databases for easy access and searches, without being integrated per se.

For example, these companies collect databases of property records, voter lists, driver's licenses, vehicle registrations, employment records, marriages, births of children, inheritances and lawsuits in which one has been engaged. Additionally, they collect everything on everyone's credit record, all credit card statements, information on schools attended and degrees held, arrest and conviction records and utility transaction records. These companies then combine these databases, or make the links between them seamless. The data becomes easy to search quickly for information on an individual. This process is an example of aggregating information and then integrating it. This is what Acxiom does, and this information is combined into dossiers of individuals' lives that are available to anyone for $50 (Behar, 2004).

Privacy advocates in the late 1990s had been alarmed at the amount and type of information that commercial and government entities were amassing on individuals. Peter Swire described the enactment of the Gramm-Leach-Bliley Act of 1999 in terms of privacy, stating that his discussion of the law would be regarded as "...placing the enactment into the context of a historical peak of privacy policy activity in the late 1990's." (Swire, 2002) Privacy advocates were concerned that the manner in which and the amount of information collected represented what was tantamount to an invasion of privacy. At the time there were calls for discussions on the appropriate manner in which to place limits on this informational aggregation and integration. More importantly, laws were passed to protect the privacy of American citizens. The Drivers Privacy Protection Act of 1994 allowed citizens to opt-out of having the information they provided to their state departments of motor vehicles (DMVs) sold. The Drivers Privacy Protection Act of 1999 made the system opt-in, i.e. citizens had the option to allow their information to be sold. States at that time then stopped selling the information. The laws survived a constitutional challenge Reno v. Condon, 528 U.S. 141 (2000). The challenge was predicated on the assertion that the Act violated the concept of federalism. The Court ruled that the prohibition of sale of driver's license information was legitimate as an exercise in regulating interstate commerce under the Commerce Clause ("The Drivers Privacy Protection Act," n.d.).

In the 1990s the government demanded that "spare keys" be developed by companies selling encryption solutions so that individuals would have no privacy in their communications. In 1998 the government had even dropped its demand that publishers of software that had encryption capability include these "spare keys" in their encryption products. In the case of encryption products, much of the pressure came from businesses.

In 2001, events changed the tenor of the discussion and the discussion of privacy took a back seat to a discussion of the supposed virtues of surveillance in The United States in contemporary American society.

Individuals in the United States are subject to surveillance and tracking technologies for various reasons with varying goals. These reasons may be partially constructed with commercial components, have national security implications and/or engage law enforcement goals. The goals would follow from the rationale; more profit in the case of commercial considerations, and security and continuity of operations in the national security and law enforcement scenarios. The government states that the goal of tracking and conducting surveillance against all of its citizens is the protection of those citizens. Central to the question regarding the use and abuse of surveillance and tracking methods and technologies is the concept of privacy.

As illustrated with the Smiths, a person might go through the day and have his or her movements and activities tracked with the aid of a variety of technologies which provide convenience but sacrifice privacy. The simple use of common devices and everyday conveniences makes almost all of the Smiths' actions and movements traceable-with or without their knowledge and certainly without their consent. Tracking and surveillance data are produced as, "by-products" of the primary "stated" purposes of the technologies.

In cases in which tracking is the central tenet of the technology, these technologies have as their primary selling point the safety of the individual. This is the case with the need to locate the source of 911 calls from cell phones, or the use of satellite tracking of vehicles for use in cases in which drivers go missing. The tracking component is sold to the consumer and in a philosophical sense to the public, under the pretense of making rescue efforts easier as well as easing the enforcement and prosecutorial efforts of law enforcement and the criminal justice system.

Government agencies, through private companies, have access to a vast amount of data about any given person. An accusation with no basis in fact is all that is required for law enforcement or the government to label a person as a terror suspect. Once an individual is labeled as a suspect or target, all of the data about an individual can be accessed by the government. Under the PATRIOT Act, there is no need for the government to have probable cause or a warrant to access dossiers. Questions of privacy and surveillance therefore revolve around the question of access to the data, by whom, and for what purpose.

The Real ID Act represents a continuation of the destruction of privacy the average American citizen faces in daily life. This loss of privacy is a danger to the average American citizen and puts the average citizen at more of a disadvantage when dealing with criminals, corporations and the government. This danger far outweighs any increase in security that Real ID could provide.

Comments by 23 experts as compiled by the Electronic Privacy Information Center (EPIC) highlight the dangers inherent in the concept and implementation of the Real ID Act from the entities listed above (criminals, corporations and government.) Identity theft will be simple with the unencrypted machine readable zones (MRZs) which provide plenty of information for identity thieves. Corporations would have a treasure trove of information regarding individuals as they were tracked throughout their daily lives swiping their Real ID card for every transaction. And as the Department of Homeland Security declared that the Privacy Act of 1974 does not apply to many components of the implementation, citizens have no way to know of or attempt to correct any inaccurate data held in the Real ID system as mandated under the Privacy Act ("Comments," 2007). Supporters of the Real ID contend that Real ID is the proper way to implement the type of secure identification that the 9/11 Commission recommended. Detractors are concerned that the implementation is insecure, that the costs are too high, that it represents an unfunded mandate to the states, and that it represents a national ID card. Americans have resisted the implementation of a national ID card every time that suggestion was floated and that it will be used for more purposes than it was originally intended ("Comments," 2007).

Adoption and use of a Real ID will impact several segments of civil society as well as attack the philosophic foundations of freedom that Americans had taken for granted. The first is the American concept of privacy and the manner in which this right was constructed from interpretations of the Bill of Rights in Supreme Court decisions. Societal norms and statutory law also have helped construct and address the societal implementation of the concept of privacy, and have helped Americans understand that concept as a birthright. These concepts include the expectation of privacy in communication, speech and association. The government changed the focus of the privacy debate in reaction to the terror of 9/11, and it has granted itself extraordinary powers to "fight terrorism."

Privacy as a Right

What is privacy and how is it a right? Most individuals have an intuitive sense of what the construct of privacy contains. In Constitutional terms, privacy is not an enumerated right, yet it is something that individuals in contemporary American society had come to expect. The effect that technology has had on privacy and people's expectations of privacy is also germane to the current societal consideration of the concept of privacy. Societal norms regarding privacy are important to consider, as the evolution of privacy as a right, and some would say, as a civil right (Radil, 1999), has progressed. The concept of privacy as a right in American society has developed historically throughout the years the Republic has been in existence as a logical extension of enumerated Constitutional rights. Of what does it consist?

Justice Brandeis famously wrote that privacy "is the right to be left alone" (Warren & Brandeis, 1890). Some contend that privacy has to do with having some measure of anonymity when one goes out in public (Slobogin, 2007).

Others might contend that it is the ability to keep information about various aspects of one's life private to various groups of people with which the individual chooses to share the information. The latter contention goes to the theory of controlling the dissemination of one's private information (Froomkin, 2000).

Based on their sense that individuals and institutions in power will seek to expand that power, the Founders ratified the first ten Amendments to the Constitution as the Bill of Rights (McWhirter & Bible, 1992). The Bill of Rights took effect in December of 1791. Among the rights enumerated in the Bill of Rights are such guarantees as the First Amendment freedom of speech, First Amendment freedom of association and assembly, Fourth Amendment freedom from unreasonable searches and seizures, Fifth Amendment rights against self-incrimination, Sixth Amendment rights to trial by jury and the right to a speedy trial and the Eighth Amendment prohibition against cruel and unusual punishment ("Bill of Rights," 1791).

These rights were grounded in the enlightened philosophies of the great European thinkers of the day and represented a breakthrough in the establishment and protection of the rights of individuals against "bad" governments. Forms of bad governments in the European tradition generally took the form of feudal and despotic governments, although the shadow of theocracy in the form of the Catholic Church and Puritanism overlay much of the theory of governance of the time (McWhirter & Bible, 1992).

Court decisions have shaped the discussion of privacy in the United States over the years. An early discussion in a law journal regarding privacy came in the form of a situation described by Warren and Brandeis regarding the making and use of an image of an individual in the public space (Warren & Brandeis, 1890) Foreshadowing the invasion of privacy by the zealotry of today's paparazzi, the authors decried the gossip-mongering of their time thus, "The press is overstepping in every direction the obvious bounds of propriety and decency. Gossip is no longer the resource of the idle and of the vicious, but has become a trade…" (Warren & Brandeis, 1890). The justices concluded that if individuals felt their privacy had been invaded, their remedy would be in the civil courts.

One of the first modern decisions regarding privacy came in the form of Griswold v Connecticut (1965) (McWhirter & Bible, 1992), which had to do with the right of individuals to practice birth control in the privacy of their own homes. "In Griswold five justices were willing to find a constitutional right to privacy, two in the 'penumbras' of the Bill of Rights, three in the Ninth Amendment… With this decision the right to privacy had finally found its way into the constitution" (McWhirter & Bible, 1992).

It is the Ninth Amendment of the Bill of Rights, which specifies: "The enumeration in the Constitution, of certain rights, shall not be construed to deny or disparage others retained by the people." ("Bill of Rights," 1791) The Ninth Amendment forms the basis for Supreme Court decisions which formalized the right to privacy. Justice Goldberg determined that to not enforce the "unenumerated" rights that the Constitution specified would "disparage" those rights (Tushnet, 2008).

In Paul v Davis (1976), an individual who had been arrested but not convicted found his name and face on a flyer distributed by the police to shopkeepers in Louisville, Kentucky, with others labeled as known shoplifters. After the charges against him had been dropped, he sued the police for invasion of privacy. Ethically, the police were in the wrong on many counts, especially in the principle of a man being innocent until proven guilty, yet Judge Rehnquist ruled against Mr. Paul because he had brought suit under the wrong theory of law; he should have sued for defamation (Parent, 1983). Thus, the law takes a narrow view of the definition of privacy and it is not necessarily in line with an intuitive understanding of privacy.

The concept of a "reasonable expectation of privacy" is a well developed concept in discussions of law. The concept of "reasonable expectation" is used in relation to discussion of what information can be gathered and used in court by law enforcement, employers, and other actors with power over the individual. The concept is developed in cases dependent on what an individual says or does, as well as the place in which the speech or action occurs, under what circumstances the speech or action occurs, and who can appropriately discover the speech or action.

The concept of "reasonable expectation of privacy" was introduced as a Fourth Amendment protection in Katz v. United States in 1967 (389 U.S. 347). The case involved the contention of the government that since a pay phone was public, bugging the phone booth without a warrant did not impinge on Fourth Amendment protections (Slobogin, 2007). The Court ruled that the Fourth Amendment protected people, not places, and that if society considered it "reasonable" that an individual was in a place and acted in a way that assumed that their actions or discussions were private, Fourth Amendment protection was implied. The Court drew the line at openly public behavior, so that any discussion in a restaurant or on a public street would not assume the guarantees of the Fourth Amendment.

The question that the courts had to address was that of what information is appropriate for various law enforcement agencies to know and how the information can be used. The general thrust inherent in defining the limits of Fourth Amendment protections has to do with what information can be legally used against an individual in a court of law.

In instances which would involve the Fourth Amendment, in the past there had to have been a probable cause finding that a crime probably had been committed, probably was being committed, or probably was about to be committed, in order for law enforcement agencies to eavesdrop or conduct other surveillance. That concept of law, however, is now considered "pre-9/11" in its thinking and application. The PATRIOT Act and subsequent additions and expansions have changed societal and legal conceptions involving what were, prior to the terror of 2001, violations of individuals' rights (Abele, 2005).

The PATRIOT Act and the accompanying Acts, as well as the guidelines under which the Federal Bureau of Investigation (FBI) operates, require no probable cause finding in order for the government to conduct surveillance against American citizens. The most recent FBI guidelines reported in the mainstream media indicate, according to Caroline Frederickson, director of the American Civil Liberties Union's (ACLU) Washington legislative office, "...the FBI will be given carte blanche to begin surveillance without factual evidence... These guidelines will lead to political witch hunts and more unwarranted investigations of political enemies and peace groups." The FBI will also be allowed to employ Counter Intelligence Program (COINTELPRO) techniques from the period that led up to the Church Committee hearings, e.g., recruiting of informants, infiltration, disguise, etc. (Johnson, 2008)

Surveillance advocates repeat as their mantra that a desire for privacy should be equated with a desire to hide some type of criminality. This is the "nothing to hide" argument for surveillance. This "nothing to hide" argument has been described as the "most common retort against privacy advocates" (Schneier, 2006, para. 1). Yet there are many instances in which criminal deceit is not reason for a person's desire for privacy, but rather an individual choice.

Throughout the history of the Republic, there has been an acknowledgement and codification of the fact that privacy exists as a right and there are classes of instances of violations of that right for which the injured parties can seek remedies through the courts. In 1905, the Georgia Supreme Court in Pavesich v. New England Life Insurance Co. concluded that a "right of privacy in matters purely private is...derived from natural law" (Solove, 2006).

Direct observation of and eavesdropping on an individual as well as availability and dissemination of information about an individual are the primary dimensions that frame the concept of individuals' privacy. These dimensions have to do with aspects of average American citizens' lives that are not criminal, but involve information that is nobody else's business, and certainly not the government's business.

Whether or not a person has cancer, or a taste for some food that may not be popular in the culture or locale (think of a vegetarian cast into small town life in cattle country in Wyoming), should and was a purely private matter, and under the Constitution and Bill of Rights, is really none of the government's business.

Conduct and speech were natural rights codified into law, and people had had protection from their neighbors pre-9/11, as well as the government. Eavesdropping was a violation of common law even in Colonial times. Eavesdropping was defined by William Blackstone in 1769 as "...listen[ing] under walls or windows, or the eaves of a house, to hearken after discourse..." (Solove, 2006).

In the years leading up to the events of 9/11/2001, the progression of privacy rights of individuals was in the direction of greater individual rights, choice and privacy. With the advent of computers and the ability to collect, store and aggregate large amounts of data, even pre-9/11, marketers were attempting to marginalize privacy rights in the quest for useful data about individuals for profit maximization. Privacy was eroded by the ability of actors with computers and databases to share information easily. Communication and tracking technologies have also served to erode individuals' privacy. And post-9/11, law enforcement and "anti-terror" considerations erased any sense of privacy and privacy rights. Commercial interests additional to defense and homeland security contractors have also driven the destruction of the concept of privacy of information.

There are no neat boundaries which can be drawn around the issues surrounding individuals' privacy and privacy rights. Privacy issues are inherently intertwined with every aspect of an individual's life, at all times during the day, every day. This is illustrated here by discussing the Smiths in their daily lives. Some aspects of the concept of privacy engage First Amendment rights, some, the Fourth Amendment.

Some rights (association and speech and search and seizure) are life and death issues under the PATRIOT Act, subsequent acts, and executive orders. The original PATRIOT Act, which has been greatly expanded with the passage of subsequent laws, allows the designation of groups as terrorist organizations. This designation can be given to groups which may be peaceful protest groups which an individual might have thought were protected by the Constitution and therefore with which they were free to associate. The use of politically motivated designation of groups as "terrorist" started with selective and politically expedient use of the designation "terrorist organization" by the State Department under the 1996 Antiterrorism Act (Cole & Dempsey, 2002).

Closer to home, the threshold for the declaring something to be "domestic terrorism" is the commission of "acts dangerous to human life that are a violation of criminal laws...[and] that appear to be intended...to influence the policy of government by intimidation or coercion." This part of the Act, written in a Minnesota state law mimicking the Act, allowed protesters who were planning actions of civil disobedience, in the spirit of the 1960s protests, to be arrested and charged with conspiracy to riot in the furtherance of terrorism in Minneapolis/St. Paul for the Republican National Convention in 2008. In this case, the citizen "terrorists" were arrested and charged preemptively, before anyone had protested anything (Goodman, 2008).

If an organization is not declared to be a "terrorist organization" but found under Section 411 of the PATRIOT Act by the Secretary of State to "undermine U.S. efforts to reduce or eliminate terrorist activities," and was shuttered under the provisions of the PATRIOT or subsequent Acts, then any individual who contributed money to that group could have his or her assets seized. Thus, under the existing laws, protesting the passage of legislation extending and expanding the USA PATRIOT Act could result in an individual's assets being forfeited due to the individual contributing money to a protest organization considered by the Secretary of State to be an organization which undermines U.S. efforts to reduce or eliminate terrorist activities. Some might argue that this circumstance represents a circumvention of the American political process (Abele, 2005). More useful for the government, this provision could easily be used instead of the "material support" provision that has been used as a pretext for raids against anti-war protesters (Gast, 2010). The seized assets would presumably include everything the anti-war protesters owned, including their cars, homes, furniture and computers.

Central to the notion of privacy is the question of whether Internet and email communications are private. Communication (speech) is a

First Amendment right and surveillance of political speech is one facet of the privacy question.

Another Constitutional question involving privacy and the Real ID Act has to do with another enumerated First Amendment right, freedom of assembly. Freedom of assembly implies the ability to move about freely (otherwise how could anyone assemble?). If one is under surveillance at all times, with all movements known and catalogued, is there a freedom to assemble?

Generally, one can consider that freedom of assembly and freedom of speech are married, as they are enumerated together in the First Amendment. If one right is abridged, intuitively, the other is also abridged. What good would it do for individuals to meet but not be able to speak freely? And conversely, what purpose would it serve to be able to speak, but not to be in personal contact with those with whom one speaks?

Due to the manner in which phone calls, emails, and all financial transactions are recorded, any attempt to donate to an organization that might attempt to safeguard citizens' rights is itself catalogued. Under a full surveillance regime, there is not even the ability to donate to an organization such as the American Civil Liberties Union (ACLU) without the government knowing. The ACLU is, as of October, 2010,, a legitimate, non-terrorist political organization. The ACLU is an impediment to the implementation of some policies of the government, however, and therefore may at some point have its membership and donor lists come under greater scrutiny and possibly be put on some type of "watch list," as WikiLeaks has been (Gamage, 2010).

WikiLeaks is a Web site which accepts and posts documents from a variety of sources. These sources are generally whistleblowers and those who are attempting to fight corruption ("About WikiLeaks," n.d.). In October, 2010, WikiLeaks posted more that 391,000 documents relating to the U.S. military's conduct of the War in Iraq of the first decade of the 2000s. A few days prior to the posting of those military documents, the United States government placed WikiLeaks on a "watch list" and the Australian government placed WikiLeaks on a blacklist.

This had the effect that the British company, Moneybookers, that handled donations to WikiLeaks stated that there were possible "money laundering" and other allegations tied to an investigation by the U.S. Government and that Moneybookers was shutting down the WikiLeaks account. The placing of WikiLeaks on the "watch list" had the effect of choking off the channel for donations which had previously been available for individuals who would support the WikiLeaks operation (Gamage, 2010). One can only assume that since WikiLeaks is a target of the Pentagon, the list of donors as well as the donors are at risk.

The Australian action is unsurprising as Australia has implemented Internet censorship on multiple occasions over the years. Australia had previously blacklisted a WikiLeaks web page about censorship (Singel, 2009).

The issue of anonymous association was addressed but not resolved in a 1972 case, Laird v. Tatum. The United States Army infiltrated and conducted domestic surveillance against groups that were planning demonstrations and peacefully airing their grievances. The Court did not address the question of privacy in one's associations. Instead, deciding that the plaintiffs had not shown that they were damaged, the Court decided that the victims of the surveillance had no standing to challenge the constitutionality of the surveillance. The Court refused to issue an injunction against the Army to stop domestic spying. Chief Justice Warren E. Burger, writing for the majority, ruled that "the 'subjective chill' that could result from fear that information collected by the government might someday be used to harm those about whom the information had been collected was not a sufficient justification to issue an injunction..." (Kuhn, 2007). However, in the dissent in 1972, Justice William O. Douglas argued that there should not be a need to show harm in order that the Court would be able to review the Army's surveillance program:

> The Bill of Rights was designed to keep agents of government and official eavesdroppers away from assemblies of people. The aim was to allow men to be free and independent and assert their rights against government. There can be no influence more paralyzing of that objective than Army surveillance. When an intelligence officer looks over every nonconformist's shoulder in the library, or walks invisibly by

his side in a picket line, or infiltrates his club, the America once extolled as the voice of liberty heard around the world no longer is cast in the image which Jefferson and Madison designed, but more in the Russian image (Kuhn, 2007).

Under scholarly definitions of terrorism, the terrorists commit terrorism in order to influence targeted governments and societies. When a targeted society or government changes in response to terrorism, the terrorists are said to have been successful. To the detriment of American citizens, in reaction to terrorists' attacks, changes have been made by the United States' government regarding citizens' freedom and privacy rights. These changes were not in the direction of greater freedom.

The Internet Age started before the terror attacks of 9/11. Discussions about privacy in the literature regarding First Amendment issues in the age of the Internet would help to frame the question of the normative privacy considerations American citizens. As members of a society governed under the laws consonant with the United States Constitution, Americans had come to expect a measure of freedom and privacy. The pre-9/11 literature on the subject demonstrates a stark contrast with the post-9/11 literature, as "anti-terror" considerations have caused the Congress and Presidents to disregard Americans' constructed privacy right, as well as other guaranteed rights under the Constitution and Bill of Rights.

Privacy in Internet Communications

Privacy considerations involving Internet communication are seen as a moving target. This is due to the fact that the Internet and its technologies are evolving rapidly (Brownlee & Claffy, 2004, Grier, 2006).

In the main, Americans have had a different attitude throughout the early history of the Republic than Europeans regarding privacy. Americans showed a preference for a greater degree of property rights-based physical privacy. This is evidenced by a societal history which includes the development of privacy-enhancing technologies. The development of barbed wire is a simple example that could be included in this category (McWhirter & Bible, 1992).

More contemporarily, the European Union had developed stricter privacy policies then the United States, especially regarding information concerning individuals, or what would be considered to be Personally Identifiable Information (PII). The U.S. has had to make guarantees to the EU regarding the manner in which information about citizens of EU countries is to be stored and disseminated (B. Sullivan, 2006) in order that U.S. corporations can do business in Europe and be trusted with data from and about European persons. Those U.S. corporations are not bound to the same level of duty of care regarding American citizens' information.

When one reads the literature describing normative attitudes about privacy from the perspective or law and jurisprudence, one finds a major focus on the Fourth Amendment. Two salient issues which have Fourth Amendment implications are FBI's Carnivore program and NSA's warrantless wiretapping program. Other issues involve Internet search results, employee expectations of privacy at work, protection of one's identity, and physical tracking (geo-location) technologies.

In the Internet age, the FBI's Carnivore program represents an invasion of privacy. No party was allowed to verify that Carnivore actually did what it claimed to do. The FBI would not allow independent review of the computer code, so no one could determine whether it was being used in the manner prescribed by law or policy (Elmore, 2001).

Another Fourth Amendment consideration includes the privacy expectations of Internet search information and it was this on which Lawless (2007) focused. Barrett (2002) discussed the FBI claims that Carnivore collected information in the manner of pen register and trap-and-trace devices. Collection of this information has implications for Fourth Amendment protections for third parties. Additionally, there is the possibility the FBI had gathered more information with Carnivore than the courts may have allowed in any given situation.

Jackson (1999) had expressed concern that the Electronic Communications Privacy Act of 1986, while providing some protection for electronic communications, did not go far enough to protect individuals' privacy in electronic communications. The Harvard Law

Review ("Keeping Secrets," 1997) was concerned with the question of striking a balance between privacy, individuals avoiding suspicionless monitoring by law enforcement, and the necessity of enforcing the law in cyberspace.

Another group of law journal articles discussed the Fourth Amendment specifically in terms of the FBI and Carnivore. Hellums (2002) is concerned with the ability of the government, through the use of Carnivore and technologies similar to Carnivore, to fulfill Justice Brandeis' prediction., made Olmstead v United States in 1928, that "...the Government, without removing papers from secret drawers, can reproduce them in court, and by which it will be enabled to expose to a jury the most intimate occurrences of the home."

Young (2001) questions the FBI's use of the laws as old as Title III of the Omnibus Crime Control and Safe Streets Act of 1968 to justify the use of Carnivore. Lincecum (2003) references the movies "The Conversation" and "Enemy of the State" in illustrating the dangers of uncontrolled eavesdropping and the general distrust Americans have of government surveillance. Another closely related article (Ditzion, 2004) concerns the use of "pen registers" and what the law says that will be applicable to the use of pen register type surveillance in the Internet age, and how they relate to "trap-and-trace" devices.

Conceptually, "pen registers" and "trap-and-trace devices" are concepts which carry forward from the circuit-switched telephone system space. A pen register detects and records numbers dialed from a phone. Trap-and-trace reveals the origin of a call that was dialed to a certain number. In terms of email, these concepts were extended to email addresses and routing information. The burden of proof for getting pen register and a trap-and-trace order was less onerous than conducting a wiretap (i.e. a Title III order). A wiretap required the burden of showing probable cause, and had time limits and other restrictions which law enforcement found to be inconvenient. For example, a Title III order "require[d] probable cause for intercepting communications' content or an ECPA order..." and "applications under Title III require the authorization of a high-level Department of Justice official and are subject to approval and review by federal district court judges" (Hellums, 2002). These requirements proved to be time-consuming for the law enforcement.

Pen register and trap-and-trace technologies are ways to implement inference tracking (E. Cole, 2003). Inference tracking involves knowing which parties are communicating with each other and can give insight into who might be up to something with some knowledge of in what activities some of the parties are known to be involved.

Carnivore was a pre-9/11 invention by the FBI which evolved out of Omnivore, which itself evolved from a "still-classified surveillance system deemed technologically deficient." (Hellums, 2002) The use or misuse of Carnivore hinged on what probable cause and court orders were necessary for its use, and the type of information to be collected. Those conducting the surveillance are purported to have the ability to set the information collection regime to various levels so that the government would collect differing amounts and types of information. Some types of discrete informational elements would be: addresses from which email was sent (to the target), email addresses to which the target sent email, address routing information (both to and from, sender and receiver) and message contents.

Some of the controversy surrounding the use of Carnivore had to do with the FBI's implausible technical explanation for the manner in which Carnivore functions. The agency assured target audiences that the FBI was not intercepting the full content of a suspect's communication when the FBI was not authorized to do so. Because the workings of Carnivore were never divulged, some thought that it was implausible that the FBI could target specific email addresses for monitoring and analysis. Carnivore had other eb:problems from civil libertarians' standpoints in terms of who would monitor the manner in which the software was installed and configured, as the software had capabilities built into it to collect all of the content information (i.e., the email message body). Carnivore also is said to possess the capability to monitor all traffic of all types (e. g., Web browsing, etc.), if the agency so desired.

In terms of the relevancy of any discussion of Carnivore per se to the present day privacy issue, there is little. The USA PATRIOT Act has obviated the need for justification of surveillance which the FBI was compelled to show in the past. Surveillance of Americans of a much more comprehensive nature is now conducted and is authorized internally by the FBI through the use of National Security Letters

(NSLs). The FBI can issue NSLs to and by itself without judicial oversight (Jordan, 2007). Post-9/11, the legal profession, as judged by the viewpoints expressed by their published representatives, was not concerned with attempting to maintain privacy in email communications.

Another discussion regarding legal issues concerning the Fourth Amendment regards the seizure of search results held at third-party search providers such as Google, Yahoo, etc. Lawless (2007) urges judicial adoption of a rights-based doctrine in upholding societal expectations of privacy for constitutional consistency. Foley (2007) notes that the court in Gonzalez v. Google stated that the government sought search information which pertained to lawful activity. That is an egregious violation of the Fourth Amendment as the prohibitions against the government "legally" obtaining information about individuals is reduced to almost zero. The trick is for the government to seek information about "suspicious activity." This dragnet for "suspicious activity" would invariably lead to revealing the search engine user's identity even if there was no previous "reasonable suspicion." This would be a violation of the Fourth Amendment.

Goldberg (2005) notes that Google is the heavyweight in the world of Web search and free email. He maintains that privacy guarantees must be maintained lest "electronic dossiers," which include records of all searches as well as all outgoing email from the free Gmail service, would be available to the government and the highest bidder.

In the aggregate, the issues discussed in these articles have to do with what expectation of privacy individuals have when conducting searches on the Internet. The search data is generally stored indefinitely at third-party search providers, such as Google. Google states openly that it never deletes any search query. Google search data has been seized and used by prosecutors. In one case, a man searched on a type of wound which he inflicted upon himself when he killed his wife and shot himself (non-fatally). The search history was evidence which ultimately proved to be his story's undoing, which was that an unknown assailant shot them and he lost consciousness (Lawless, 2007). That type of case may be highly nuanced, and it easy to rationalize any shortcuts as having the ends justify the means.

Lawless makes note of the tests that the courts apply when deciding if a "reasonable expectation of privacy" has any basis in any given situation. The courts generally tie this expectation to societal norms and precedents of guarantees the courts provide for individuals. Applying "reasonable expectation" applies to search data results in the conundrum that because third-party search providers do nothing to protect the queries entered into the search engine, "it (doing nothing to protect the privacy of search queries and results) reinforces the privacy norms of a politically and temporally insulated judiciary: once people know their searches are exposed, then – by the time these cases are contested – there will, in truth, be no expectation of privacy" (Lawless, 2007).

Almost no law review articles discuss or describe litigation concerning the USA PATRIOT Act. The fact that an individual must have standing (a legal term of art meaning they have to have some kind of interest caused by having been directly affected by the law) to sue limits the type and number of cases which can be brought by victims of application of the Act. These victims are not allowed, under the terms of application of the Act, to speak about the fact that they have had their Constitutional rights violated. They have no attorneys representing them as the courts are secret. Those snatched under the Act can be held incommunicado with no habeas corpus. A victim of application of the Act could sue on the basis that application of the Act was a violation of that individual's Constitutional rights, if that individual would be able to see a judge. But without habeas corpus, the victim may never see a judge or an attorney.

The government contends that any application of the Act is a secret affair. If an individual divulges the fact that they aided law enforcement in the execution of any order under the Act, that individual can be arrested under provisions of the same Act and just disappear. The secret arrest and secret incarceration with no judge and no jury make judicial review of the constitutionality of the Act moot. If no one who has been affected by the Act can show that they have standing then no one who can petition a court for a redress of grievances, i.e. that they were harmed. The target, the investigation and the harm are kept secret. The government's claim that the plaintiff lacked standing led to the dismissal of a case in Cincinnati in July 2007. The court stated that the plaintiffs in the case, including lawyers and journalists, could not prove they had been subject to surveillance and therefore could not show injury, and therefore did not have standing to sue (Liptak, 2007).

Another tactic the government uses to keep issues out of court is to claim that there is some type of prejudicial harm that can come to security efforts if a judge were to hear cases that involve secrecy and/or national security. This is the tactic the government tried to use in the case of Al-Haramain v. Bush in the United States District Court for the Northern District of California. Al-Haramain was not specifically about the PATRIOT Act, but demonstrated that occasionally the government's usual declaration of harm to national security as a way to keep illegal government activity from being addressed in court is not always accepted as an excuse by the judiciary.

Al-Haramain was a civil case, heard in court only because of a mistake by the government. A favorable ruling from a federal judge that evidence based on the plaintiff's attorneys' memories was sufficient for the case to move forward. Al-Haramain addressed the warrantless wiretapping that was conducted against American citizens by the NSA and national security apparatus.

Al-Haramain was a charity that now is no more. It was shut down for suspicion of being involved in financing terrorists and terrorism. Joe Eisenberg argued on the side of the charity which claimed it had been given copies of its phone logs by the Treasury Department by accident. The papers Treasury turned over were marked "Top Secret" on each page. The FBI retrieved the packet of papers, but not before several people in the law office had seen them.

When the warrantless surveillance program was revealed in the press in December 2005, the attorneys for the charity realized what they had seen was evidence generated from warrantless wiretaps and they filed suit (Elias, 2007). The government argued that "The Document," as it is referred to in court papers, should not be entered into evidence or produced through discovery, as it was a state secret. The court let the suit proceed based on the recollection of a plaintiff who had seen it. The government argued that the only way to verify if the recollection was correct was to compare it to The Document, but since The Document would not be produced, the suit should be dismissed.

The Deputy Solicitor General Gregory Garre, in urging the judges to dismiss the lawsuit, said that exposing The Document, or even continuing with the case, would jeopardize the national security of the United States. When challenged as to whether the judiciary should just take the executive branch's word that something should be considered a state secret, Garre suggested that the courts should show the "utmost deference" to the Bush administration (Poulsen, 2007).

The lengths to which the government had gone to try to maintain the secrecy of The Document, notwithstanding the episode of the Department of the Treasury handing it over to the subject of their investigation, were extreme. Plaintiff's Attorney Jon Eisenberg was forced to type his briefs on a government computer with an armed guard watching, could not keep copies of what he'd written, and any printouts he made were mandated to be taken for shredding by the guard. As he wrote in an email:

> So, it's like this. Yesterday, under the auspices and control of my litigation adversaries, at their offices and on their computer, I wrote a brief, of which I was not allowed to keep a copy, responding to arguments which I was not permitted to see, which will be met by a reply which I will not be permitted to see. (Liptak, 2007)

A three-judge panel in a Washington appeals court did not agree with the government's approach to handling cases involving state secrets. Judge Judith W. Rogers, for the majority, wrote that the deck seemed stacked for the government in that when a plaintiff "lacks information about his claim, the complaint must be dismissed... But as soon as any information is acquired, it becomes too risky to introduce the evidence at trial" (Liptak, 2007).

In the Al-Haramain case, the government made a motion to dismiss in January, 2009 and it was denied. ("Order Pertaining to Al-Haramain," 2009) There was a conference scheduled for January 23, 2009. ("Clerk's Notice," 2009) At that time the government was ordered to produce a plan by February 13, 2009 for going forward with the case, bearing in mind the sensitivity of the documents the court needed to see. On February 11 the government filed a brief with the court declaring its intention to appeal and get a stay. The court found that the decision to move forward with the case was not a decision which the government could appeal. Judge Walker issued an order dated February 13, 2009, denying the government's motion to appeal and stay the court's order that the government produce the documents in camera that the court has determined that it must see in order to proceed with the case.

On March 31, 2010, United States District Chief Judge Vaughn R. Walker issued the order for the plaintiffs granting summary judgment on the issue of the defendants' liability under FISA ("CaseM: 06-cv-01791-VRW Document721," 2010). The government had conducted surveillance against the charity without obtaining the proper FISA warrant to conduct the surveillance. The government had ample opportunity to produce the warrant but did not do so, and fought every step of the way to avoid admitting that it had acted illegally. Then, after the judgment had been entered, the government fought against even the payment of attorney's fees for the attorneys who won the case against the government ("Case3: 06-md-01791-VRW Document748," 2010).

Other cases involving the warrantless wiretapping are still making their ways through the court system. One of these is Jewel v. NSA.

As of October, 2010, an appeal of the District Court decision was filed in Jewel v. NSA. In this case, the plaintiffs seek to stop the wholesale surveillance being conducted by AT&T on their customer and to stop AT&T from turning over their customers' communications and communications records to NSA. The District Court decision, signed by the same Judge Walker who had found for the plaintiffs in Al-Haramain, found that the plaintiffs in Jewel had no standing because they had only a "generalized grievance." The judge had cited the 2005 decision in the DC Circuit Court in Seegers v. Gonzalez, that "[I]njuries that are shared and generalized – such as the right to have the government act in accordance with the law – are not sufficient to support standing," ("CaseM: 06-cv-01791-VRW Document703," 2010, p. 3).

The opening brief in the appeal notes that, "Unless corrected, the District Court's ruling risks creating a perverse incentive for the government to violate the privacy rights of as many citizens as possible in order to avoid judicial review of its actions," ("Case: 10-15616 ID: 7439555," 2010, p. 3).

Another case that is central to the warrantless wiretapping question is Hepting vs. AT&T . The Electronic Freedom Foundation (EFF) had been making inroads in court against NSA warrantless wiretapping with this lawsuit. In response, the Congress passed the Foreign Intelligence Surveillance Act Amendments Act (FISAAA) and on July 10, 2008, President Bush signed it into law as Public Law 110-208. With that law in place, almost all of the cases against telecoms as carriers who conducted the wiretapping of American citizens without warrants, were dismissed under Section 802 of FISAAA ("Case M: 06-cv-01791-VRW Document 639," 2009).

Two classes of suit were not covered under Section 802. The first class involved suits brought by the United States against states attorneys general, which would be subject to summary judgment in a separate order under Section 803. These suits were brought by the United States to stop investigations and quash subpoenas issued by states attorneys general who were attempting to investigate on behalf of the people of their state the federal government's actions in wiretapping American citizens without any court orders. Summary judgment was granted as Section 803 of the FISAAA states, ""[n]o state shall have authority to ... conduct an investigation into ... [or] require ... the disclosure of information about ... an electronic communication service provider's alleged assistance to an element of the intelligence community." ("E-Commerce Law Week, Issue 560," 2009, para. 2)

The second class of suit not dismissed were those against government entities, such as Al-Haramain, and these suits were allowed to proceed. Suits against the government and government actors were not prohibited under the FISAAA and that fact was specifically cited in Judge Walker's order to dismiss the suits that were covered ("Case M: 06-cv-01791-VRW Document 639," 2009).

Dixon (1997) describes the privacy situation in the early days of the commercial Internet, and addressed employers' monitoring of employees' email communication. The use of email in the corporate environment was relatively new, and employees generally were under the impression that their expectation of privacy was similar in using email as to that expectation of privacy in making personal phone calls.

The court ruled in Smythe v Pillsbury, decided in the United States District Court for the Eastern District of Pennsylvania, January 18, 1996, that employee email had no privacy protection. Dixon takes issue with this decision, maintaining that the court misread the societal expectation of privacy, and that from a culturally normative viewpoint, the employees should have been able to expect their email communications to be treated as private, much as personal phone calls in the workplace were protected.

According to Dixon, there existed an expectation of privacy in a wider sense. On the other side of the normative coin, the federal court's decision "is significant because it is the first federal decision to hold that a private sector at-will employee has no right of privacy in the contents of his or her email when it is sent over an employer's email system" (Dixon, 1997). Dixon's argument is that if the employer gives the employee access to the public Internet via the company network, and that employee uses some type of Web-based mail system, that employee has some expectation of privacy.

Another issue involving reasonable expectation of privacy and probable cause involves wiretapping. Courts had avoided addressing the constitutional issues surrounding wiretapping for 40 years. Two cases in 1967, Katz v. United States and Berger v. New York, established procedural safeguards to be placed on traditional wiretaps based on Fourth Amendment considerations. Since that time, however, the courts have not subjected modern electronic surveillance practices to constitutional scrutiny (Freiwald, 2007).

What are normative attitudes about privacy and what are the unanswered questions about government surveillance as it relates to the Constitution? The first case challenging, on constitutional grounds, the Stored Communications Act (SCA), Warshak v. United States. was pending in the Sixth Circuit at the time of Freiwald's journal article going to publication (Freiwald, 2007).

The SCA was passed as a subset of the Electronic Communications Privacy Act (ECPA) in 1986.

Freiwald hypothesizes as to the reason that there has been no constitutional review of any of this warrantless invasion of privacy by the government. She gives the reason simply as the fact that a test for users' reasonable expectation of privacy needs to be applied for the courts to rule on these issues, and that this is beyond the capability of the courts, in that they "lack adequate empirical data for the positive inquiry and adequate guidance for the normative one" (Freiwald, 2007).

Subsequent to Freiwald's examination of the issue, the court did come down on the side of privacy, but only in that the police need search warrants to seize emails from ISPs. These warrants would be issued on the showing of probable cause. The government could also issue subpoenas in a bid to conduct a "constructive search." The issuance of a subpoena means that the target of the seizure would be able to go to court to challenge the seizure. From the perspective of the general public, it was a good decision for privacy advocates because it limited the ability of the government to engage in warrantless fishing expeditions ("Warshak v. United States," 2007).

The case of Senior Chief Petty Officer Timothy McVeigh of the U.S. Navy involved the disclosure of his online identity to the U.S. Navy. The Navy investigated the sexual orientation of whoever had a certain screen name on AOL. McVeigh was associated with his screen name by AOL employees in direct contravention of the company policy of non-disclosure of information about their subscribers (McTigue, 1999). McVeigh was dismissed from the Navy because of the company having disclosed his identity in violation of its own stated policies.

A major issue in the study and discussion of the government intercepting, storing and reading American citizens' emails has to do with the fact that the state bars had not decided whether attorney-client communication could occur via email without encryption. The bars' confusion as to the standard of confidentiality to which client communications should have been kept appeared to fly in the face of knowledge the state bars should have had regarding the problem for their clients knowing that law enforcement copies and seizes stored emails (McTigue, 1999).

McTigue posits a reason for the legal community's naiveté concerning the difference between stored communication and intercepted communication in terms of maintaining attorney-client privilege. This naiveté involves the fact that state bar associations focused on Title I of the ECPA which applies to email interception. In real-time, email interception is as difficult legally as wiretapping in that law enforcement used to need a warrant (that has changed with the

PATRIOT Act.) Title II of the ECPA applies to the stored email (and data). Despite the fact that it is illegal to disclose stored information in an unauthorized fashion, with the "proper authorization," the attorney-client privilege cannot be maintained against the state without the use of some type of cryptographic protective measure. Title I is not relevant when it comes to the government seizing the stored communication per Title II (McTigue, 1999) and in non-technical circles, this could lead to confusion.

Cell phones are able to connect to any cell tower and hand the calls off as the owner of the phone travels. Global Positioning Systems (GPS) can be turned around and used to plot the location of anyone using these technologies at any time. These records are stored by the entities providing the services, and are considered "contentless" data. The question with these technologies has to do with whether a person has a reasonable expectation of privacy of location when employing these technologies.

Glancy (1995) correctly identified the future issue of geo-location data being stored at service providers. The near ubiquitous adoption of the technologies which provide geo-location data put everyone's movements into databases for possible future retrieval.

Caldwell (2006) argues the case for privacy very specifically from the point of view of the Florida Constitution. Specifically, the clause in Article I, Section 23 ("Florida Constitution," 1968) enumerates the right to be left alone. This Right to Privacy enumerated in the Florida Constitution parallels Fourth Amendment protection and is synchronous with the pre-9/11 federal interpretation of what the Fourth Amendment really means.

Caldwell examines whether there is an expectation of privacy regarding cellular calls under the conditions of the 'Shaktman test.' This is a three part test to determine if a user has a reasonable expectation of privacy. This test is stated as: "...the state carries the burden of satisfying the three-part test of compelling state interest, relevance, and least intrusive means" ("Limbaugh v. Florida," 2004). The Limbaugh case, in the post-PATRIOT Act age, concerned Rush Limbaugh's medical records, which Limbaugh's attorneys contended were seized illegally from four of Limbaugh's physicians. In the Limbaugh investigation, the PATRIOT Act was not invoked. If it were, the Act specifies that in terrorism investigations (and remember that under the PATRIOT Act almost anything can be classified as "terrorism") the state can seize and use medical records without probable cause or a search warrant – that all the state must do is claim that those records are germane to some investigation (Lenzer, 2006).

Another technology that Caldwell examines is implicated in the example of Kyllo v United States. In this case, the police used thermal imaging to detect drug activity inside a home. The Supreme Court argued that the police could not specifically use "sense-enhancing" technologies against random targets, or targets they intend to examine without a warrant, unless those techniques were in widespread use by the general public (Caldwell, 2006). Unfortunately for privacy considerations of the general public, the cost of technology continues to go down, and therefore the chance of interpreting something as being in "widespread use" increases.

Glancy (1995) posited specifically the type of situation in which the logical conclusion is that each person ultimately would have to register their destination every time they were about to leave to go somewhere. Ostensibly, this type of surveillance system would determine which roads upon which the user would drive. The corollary of the use of this technology would also allow for constant monitoring of the individual's location, which we now have fifteen years later. The results of this monitoring would be stored in a database and correlated with the patterns given to private industry for more targeted marketing, and in the post-9/11 age, government.

Phillips (2005) discusses the set up and implementation of the E9-1-1 system in Texas, and how the raw geo-location data could be used to build profiles of individuals who were being tracked. A simple move would be to say that the government would have access to geo-location data and be able to build location/identity databases for any reason, of which one could be anti-terrorism tracking. Anti-terrorism would not be the only use.

There have been differing rulings as to the question of whether the government can seize cell phone location records and/or get real time cell phone location data without a warrant. As recently as 2005, there were differing opinions in federal courts in terms of what Fourth Amendment protections applied to those data. In five cases in 2005, two judges treated the request for real time data as an order for a tracking device, two treated them as wiretaps and another held it was the same as a pen register order (the order with the least protection for the target). This part of the law is still evolving ("Government Requests," 2006).

Americans' Attitudes Regarding Privacy

Davis and Silver (2004) conducted a survey in the aftermath of the 9/11 attacks. The telephone survey was conducted between November 14, 2001 and January 15, 2002 and surveyed 1,448 respondents.

There were nine questions on which the research conclusions were predicated. The answers to these questions indicated the respondent's choice between preferring security and preferring civil liberties.

The questions postulated situations in which the respondent had to make a choice and the responses organized in tabular form. In the case of the "Give up some civil liberties" entry in the table, the respondents were asked if they would be willing to give up some civil liberties if it would make the country safer. If the respondent answered yes, the respondent would be categorized for that question as preferring security to civil liberties. For the table entry for results for "Crime to belong to a terrorist organization," the question was posed and the answer categorized in the following way:

> In [the] Survey, when the value trade-off is framed as the need to be safe and secure against judging people guilty by association – "people who belong to or associate with terrorist organizations should be considered a terrorist" – 71% support treating people as guilty based on their associations (Davis & Silver, 2004, p. 32).

When questions such as "Warrantless searches on suspicion" and "Monitor telephone and email" were posed, the respondents were lukewarm to these ideas as solutions to the nations "security" problem. Even in the initial post-9/11 hysteria and fear, most people voted to protect civil liberties the majority of the time. Additionally, "Investigate protesters" received only 8% agreement for a security response, with 92% taking the civil liberties side. This is in line with Chomsky's observation that those who make policy and are in charge of both political parties are to the right of the populations they "serve" (Chomsky & Matta, 2008).

Warrantless searches received only 23% approval, and monitoring telephone and email received only 34% agreement in terms of the security responses. Thus it is evident via this self-reporting survey mechanism that the societal norm in American's minds is an inclination toward maintaining a free society even in the immediate aftermath of a terrorist attack (Davis & Silver, 2004). We can conclude that immediately after the attacks of 9/11, the American public was only slightly in favor of giving up some of their civil liberties in return for security. In regards to anti-war protest groups, Americans did not favor suppressing political dissent.

Even though events of 9/11 seemed to change the focus of the discussion regarding privacy, Americans still favored having privacy in a legal sense and were not inclined to give up all of their rights. The normative cultural values of Americans regarding privacy did not change, and Americans wanted to keep what they thought they had of it. However, the playing field for privacy rights tilted so much in favor of the government that it seems to have become difficult for scholars and privacy advocates to decide about which privacy destroying initiatives to write because there were so many.

Post-9/11, the standards the government had to meet and the requirements necessary for safeguarding privacy and civil rights changed overnight with the passage of the USA PATRIOT Act and the other acts complementing it. This legislation and other bills like it changed the tone of the privacy debate. Privacy and civil rights advocates were put on the defensive and had to start their defense of Americans' rights from a starting point much further away from reasonable positions.

The right to privacy had been built up over the years by degrees with court rulings establishing and expanding the right of American citizens to have some measure of protection of their privacy from corporations and the government. Strict constitutionalists could reasonably maintain that the right to privacy existed and that there was no need to establish the right to privacy because the Constitution didn't grant the federal government the power to decide if American citizens should or should not have privacy.

The main battlegrounds in the privacy war had been battles over email seizure, email monitoring, Web surfing and location tracking and the associated profiling which the organization of all of the data about an individual would yield. The new battlegrounds are going to be those over constant surveillance on streets and highways, surveillance of what citizens read, write and think, and even the question of whether Americans have any privacy when on or in their private property; their homes, ranches, farms and back yards.

Americans still want and value their privacy. However, there are now serious problems for those who care about personal privacy and liberty. This has been brought about by the manner in which the government conducts surveillance, and who the government puts under surveillance.

Privacy and the Law

The events of September 11, 2001 were cited as the reason which precipitated the passage of laws which have become flashpoints in the discussion regarding privacy. Intelligence and law enforcement agencies had been instructed to shift their efforts toward prevention of terrorism. This change in counter-terror strategy was in contrast with previous efforts to apprehend and prosecute terrorists after the terrorist act has been committed. The new laws which allowed or required constant surveillance of American citizens were the tools the government claimed were necessary to conduct the surveillance necessary to combat terrorism.

The Uniting and Strengthening America by Providing Appropriate Tools Required to Intercept and Obstruct Terrorism (USA PATRIOT) Act of 2001 is the cornerstone of the new set of laws which were enacted in response to the perceived terrorist threat. The Act was signed into law on October 26, 2001 (*Report From the Field*, 2004) The Act has subsequently been renewed, with revisions and expansion of the government's powers, as there were some sunset provisions in the Act as a protection for civil liberties.

Those sunset provisions were nullified by the provisions of the Act which were extended and expanded with the signing of H.R. 2417 "Intelligence Authorization Act for Fiscal Year 2004" (G. Bush, 2003) on December 13, 2003, HR 3199 "USA PATRIOT Improvement and Reauthorization Act of 2005" on March 13, 2006, and S2271 "USA PATRIOT Act Additional Reauthorizing Amendments Act of 2006" on the same day (G. Bush, 2006).

The earlier laws were precursors to the Real ID Act, which was signed into law on May 11, 2005. The laws signed after 2005, which continued the trend of increasing the power of government, can all be considered to be cut from the same cloth, including the FISA Amendments Act of 2008, Public Law 110-261.

The sections of the laws of concern here relate to the expanded powers the government granted to its intelligence and law enforcement agencies for surveillance of and all individuals, citizen or not, within the United States. Under these laws the government can conduct surveillance with little or no oversight and in many cases without any judicial review.

The lack of judicial review is a theme in literature regarding Fourth Amendment rights and the tradition of 'probable cause' The Fourth Amendment is the amendment which proscribes "unreasonable searches and seizures."

> The right of the people to be secure in their persons, houses, papers, and effects, against unreasonable searches and seizures, shall not be violated, and no Warrants shall issue, but upon probable cause, supported by Oath or affirmation, and particularly describing the place to be searched, and the persons or things to be seized ("Bill of Rights," 1791).

The full text of the Fourth Amendment is included here to demonstrate that as technology has evolved, the language of the Constitution must be interpreted according to the intent of those who framed the Constitution for this amendment to remain relevant. This is referred "original intent" in that the framer's had intended some specific goals of the documents when they wrote the Constitution and Bill of Rights and thus, whatever "progress" had occurred, technologically or in a social science sense, would still fall within the scope of the vision of the Founders.

Application of the USA PATRIOT Act also has Fifth Amendment (right against self-incrimination) ramifications. Additional fallout from the Global War on Terror (GWOT – this is an operational term used by the Defense Department to describe operations against terrorism) include possible Sixth Amendment (speedy trial, right to confront accuser) and Eighth Amendment (cruel and unusual punishment) issues.

The use of these laws infringes on the First Amendment rights of individuals, and leads directly to the abridgement of rights that the Real ID Act represents. The Real ID Act was passed ostensibly to provide a framework requiring verification of identity of U.S. persons and therefore ostensibly providing security for the society at large. The idea of a guarantee of security being tied to the guarantee of identity of individuals carrying these Real IDs is specious.

What the use of Real IDs will mostly accomplish will be to establish a single point of identity for tracking citizens throughout their daily lives. Tracking citizens will become even easier than it is currently. The initial Real ID RFID specification mandated that citizens' information is stored on chip the card in unencrypted form. Additionally, the current specification and implementation of "enhanced drivers' licenses" (EDLs) requires no security features. In this way, anyone with an RFID reader can read the information on the EDL. DHS had previously dismissed security concerns about the EDL and Real ID security flaws as an academic exercise, and had stated the department will do nothing to enhance the security in the specification of the Real ID and EDLs.

A security researcher debunked that bit of disinformation by driving around San Francisco harvesting EDLs and passport numbers using $250 of commercial off the shelf (COTS) technology. According to the researcher, he wanted to provide the proof-of-concept demonstration (Goodin, 2009). This lack of security of the information on the IDs may seem counterintuitive, yet the manner in which the Real IDs are specified provides that the data be stored in plain text. The original specification was for RFID, although that specification changed over time and is not the mechanism for the implementation of the machine readable zone (MRZ). However, according to the wide latitude enjoyed by DHS under the law, there is nothing to keep DHS from specifying the RFID implementation in the future. The current rules dictate a 2D bar code on the actual ID card and a massive distributed database. Each state must maintain a database of Real ID information, and allow interconnections to other states for database queries (Minimum Standards, 2008)

The Public Discourse and Societal Norms Regarding Privacy

The right to privacy, although not written into the Constitution, was derived from reading the intent of the Constitution by various Supreme Courts and formed the basis for decisions rendered based on those readings. Thus the rights to privacy are built on fundamental rights of the people guaranteed in the Constitution.

The largest shift in the nature of the public discourse regarding privacy occurred with an incident of international terrorism. The U.S. Government stated the need to protect its citizens and itself from international and domestic terrorists. In the United States, the events of 9/11 were the catalyst for major changes in the way privacy was regarded and implemented ("USA Patriot Act," 2001)

Prior to 9/11, there had been serious discussion within the computer profession regarding the manner in which individuals' information should be handled by the government and commercial entities. Industry actors acted according to a rational choice (for corporate actors) model when it came to the collection and use of individuals' information. The corporate actors would attempt to maximize the profit realized from collecting and brokering the personal information they collected, while doing the minimum possible to safeguard the information. Milberg (1995) examined the issues and concluded that corporate actors would do well to protect the information of the individuals whose information they collected, lest citizen and consumer concern trigger some level of regulatory remedy. They also found an overriding consideration that should have been applied-that information privacy could be considered a "hypernorm," transcending cultures and a fundamental element of human existence -

thereby creating an ethical imperative for the information's protection (Milberg et al., 1995).

Another concern was that an individual has little control individuals can exercise over their information once it is in a database. Froomkin's (2000) initial solution was that individuals should attempt to limit the amount of information they disclose to marketers and the government. Froomkin discusses the impediment to expecting individuals to attempt to safeguard their privacy as the "media-sanctioned exhibitionism and voyeurism" in society (Froomkin, 2000, p. 1466). He observes that some might think it reactionary to worry about information privacy under these circumstances.

Various types of privacy-destroying technologies are those which "facilitate the acquisition of raw data and those that allow one to process and collate that data in interesting ways" (Froomkin, 2000, p. 1468). Data can be collected in a variety of ways. Data can be collected for a single purpose and not associated with an individual, such as an anonymous customer survey. Or data can be collected and associated with an individual, such as supermarket purchases associated with a loyalty card. The latter type of data, that which can be associated with an individual, can provide the foundation for or additional information to aid in the development of personal profiles.

In the endgame of information acquisition, the questions of prediction and predictive abilities are paramount. This is the case with the NSA's "Advanced QUestioning Answering for INTelligence," or Aquaint program (Bamford, 2008). Aquaint is the most advanced and modern profiling and prediction tool possessed by the agency. NSA also has, especially for the warrantless wiretapping aspect of the operation, a slew of social network analysis, data mining and traffic analysis tools. All of these need information as input, but the tools aggregate and analyze the data (Bamford, 2008), associating it with specific individuals and building profiles, in the manner that Froomkin described in his pre-9/11 work.

Post September 11, policies regarding privacy would take two roads simultaneously. The first road involved the continuation of the public discussion regarding privacy in the sense that it had been conducted pre-9/11 in terms of local law enforcement and commercial interests. The second road involved the discussion of privacy in the context of anti-terrorism and national security.

An example of the post-9/11 privacy concern, as well as the public (government)-private surveillance partnership, is illustrated in the case of Lakehead University in Thunder Bay, Ontario. In this case, concerns over the PATRIOT Act and the powers of the U.S. government to harvest data off servers in the United States made faculty at the university wary of the use of Google's products and services.

Michael Pawlowski, vice president of administration and finance, defended the university's decision to allow Google to build out a new email and collaborative tool system for the university, at no cost to Lakehead. The downside was that the system could not be used to transmit any private data, including students' grades. The PATRIOT Act gives the U.S. Government the authority to "secretly view data held by U.S. organizations." (Avery, 2008) This type of activity is contrary to Canadian privacy laws, which requires individuals to be notified when their data is shared and also that organizations protect individuals' data.

Tom Puk, a former president of the faculty association at Lakehead, elaborated on the grievance that the faculty association filed with the university, saying, "By getting this free from Google, they gave away our rights" (Avery, 2008). Darren Meister, associate professor of information systems at the Richard Ivey School of Business, observing the disconnect between Canada's privacy laws and the United States' security measures, noted that in terms of Canadian organizations making the decision to allow their data to reside on U.S. servers, "You have to decide which law you are going to break" (Avery, 2008).

As Mr. Puk observed, the PATRIOT Act allows the DHS to examine all of the information held on the servers it can find, and then build profiles based on the writings found there. This could be a problem for academic freedom in Mr. Puk's estimation, as individuals might be researching something that might end up getting them disqualified for entry into the U.S. (Avery, 2008). Various academics and researchers have been denied entry to the U.S. even as they were scheduled to give conference presentations, so the fear is not entirely groundless (Keizer, 2007).

Google maintains that it makes valiant efforts to protect customer records, although some observers would debate that point. Specifically its policies on anonymization of user data allow the user data association to be easily recovered in one step (Metz, 2008). Google has also provided the Center for Disease Control (CDC) geo-location data based on IP address and data regarding user searches to help the U.S. government locate flu outbreaks (Helft, 2008).

Government's Assumption of Extraordinary Power

In times of war and national emergency the U.S. Congress had passed laws that restricted personal liberty for national security reasons. Enforcement of these laws can be seen as abridgements to and restrictions of enumerated rights, including such First Amendment rights as the freedoms of speech, assembly and association.

Wartime has also been used as the reason for using a conceptually different framework for deciding the manner in which crime and punishment are defined. For example, during World War II, military tribunals for foreign enemy combatants were instantiated and their legality upheld by the Supreme Court in Johnson v. Eisentrager (Posner, 2006).

The issues of crime and punishment in times of the abridgement of enumerated Constitutional rights directly relate to privacy in terms of the First Amendment as a protection against privacy-destroying surveillance. For example, during World War I, the government encouraged citizens to report on their fellow citizens in cases of speech or action that might be interpreted as disloyalty to the government.

As most speech was legal, even under the terms of the wartime laws, Fourth Amendment guarantees against unreasonable search and seizure were violated. Individuals speaking privately to another private individual (i.e., not law enforcement personnel), who were then reported to law enforcement for speech that was not illegal, had had their Fourth Amendment rights violated. Then by extension, in cases in which three or more individuals gathered, the privacy and enumerated right destroying nature of these extraordinary powers also infringed on the enumerated First Amendment right of freedom of assembly.

Alien and Sedition Acts

The first instance of legislating restrictions on personal freedom due to national emergency occurred in 1798 with the passage of the Alien and Sedition Acts. These consisted of the Naturalization Act, the Alien Friends Act, the Alien Enemies Act and the Sedition Act.

Europe was in the throes of war, with the countries of France and England at war with each other. The United States was reluctant to join the conflict on either side, hoping to remain neutral. However, the French claimed that the Americans were trading with Britain and seized and sank American merchant ships. That time in American history has been characterized as an undeclared naval war with France (Smelser, 1954).

The Alien Friends Act was enacted because the government was afraid that non-citizens (aliens) might be disloyal and therefore these aliens represented a danger to the Republic. The Alien Act gave the President power to detain and deport any non-citizen who was considered to possibly pose a danger to the United States ("Alien Act of 1798," 1798).

The Sedition Act of 1798 prohibited the publication of "any false, scandalous, and malicious writing" against the government of the United States or the institutions of the Executive or legislature. Enforcement of this Act could be seen as a prima facie abridgement of First Amendment freedoms. The Sedition Act was successfully used to prosecute political dissidents who were labeled as such by the Adams administration. The Act expired on John Adams' last day in office and Jefferson pardoned those who had been convicted under the Act (Stone, 2003).

The Civil War – Habeas Corpus

The Civil War led to some abridgements of traditional protections under the law in the name of national security. A notable example of this abridgement was the suspension of the writ of habeas corpus.

President Abraham Lincoln, soon after taking office in 1861, had considered and then rejected the idea of preventing the Maryland state legislature from meeting on April 26th. There was a legitimate concern that Maryland would vote to secede from the Union, thereby isolating Washington, D.C. (Halbert, 1958).

Soon after hostilities started with the attack on Fort Sumter, the Sixth Massachusetts Volunteers were attacked by a mob of Confederate sympathizers as they marched through Baltimore on their way to the capital. The Massachusetts militia arrived in Washington on the 19th of April. The attack by the mob and the subsequent rioting left sixteen dead and there was much damage to the city. The mayor of Baltimore then ordered the destruction of the bridges connecting Baltimore to the Union to prevent more Union troops from entering the city (Stone, 2003).

Under these circumstances, President Lincoln was still reluctant to suspend habeas corpus, yet in a strategic sense he decided he had to take steps to prevent Maryland from seceding. The President decided to wait and see what the legislature of the state of Maryland would do. However, in case the legislators did decide to secede, the President declared in orders to General Winfield Scott on April 25th, 1861, General Scott should bombard their cities "if necessary," and "in the extremest necessity," suspend the writ of habeas corpus. Maryland never seceded so that order did not need to be carried out (Halbert, 1958).

On April 27th, President Lincoln ordered the suspension of the writ of habeas corpus along the line of the military front, drawn from Philadelphia and Washington, via Perryville, Annapolis City and Annapolis Junction. It was in this area that John Merryman operated (Halbert, 1958).

John Merryman had raised a company of soldiers for the Confederates and started drilling them. Merryman and these recruits were in possession of arms and Merryman was thus committing treason. On May 25, 1861, Merryman was arrested for "various acts of treason..." and held at Fort McHenry (Halbert, 1958). Merryman filed a writ of habeas corpus, and the petition was assigned to Chief Justice Robert Taney, a strict constitutionalist from the south, who ruled in Merryman's favor, i.e., ruling that only Congress had the authorization to suspend habeas corpus, and therefore President Lincoln's orders were illegal. The President ignored the Court. The New York Times attacked Justice Taney for making an "officious and improper" decision as it "presents the ungracious spectacle" of the judge wishing to "exculpate a traitor" (Stone, 2003).

President Lincoln explained his rationale for suspending the writ by stating famously that Judge Taney's decision would allow "all the laws, but one, to go unexecuted, and the Government itself go to piece, lest that one be violated." A few weeks later, the President suspended the writ in Florida.

President Lincoln suspended the writ of habeas corpus on eight separate occasions, including the most extreme suspension order, a nationwide suspension which declared that "[A]ll persons...guilty of any disloyal practice...shall be subject to martial law." In 1863, the Congress legislated the President's actions into law. The Democratic press widely quoted William Seward when Seward told the British minister in Washington that, "I can touch a bell on my right hand and order the arrest of a citizen in Ohio. I can touch the bell again and order the imprisonment of a citizen of New York, and no power on earth but that of the President can release them. Can the Queen of England, in her dominions, say as much?" (Stone, 2003)

After the war, the writ of habeas corpus was restored.

World War I – The Espionage and Sedition Acts

In April 1917, the United States entered the war in Europe and public opinion was divided as to whether the United States should participate in the war in Europe. Many citizens believed the motives behind the United States' entry into the war were less than pure, and that the United States was going to war to protect wealthy individuals' investments. Nebraska Senator Frank Norris said, "[W]e are about to put a dollar sign upon the American flag." President Woodrow Wilson was not of the mind to allow this type of dissent. He declared that disloyalty "must be crushed out" and that disloyal individuals "had sacrificed their right to civil liberties" (Stone, 2003).

The Espionage Act of 1917 was primarily concerned with espionage and sabotage. Other provisions of the Act had consequences for free speech. Specifically, any speech of the nature that could be considered to obstruct recruiting or enlistment in the armed forces was restricted. Anti-war speech and dissent regarding governmental policy was therefore considered to be an attempt to discourage enlistment. Attorney General Charles Gregory declared in November 1917, referring to those who dissented regarding the war, "May God have mercy on them, for they need expect none from an outraged people and an avenging government." (Stone, 2003)

Initially, as prosecutions under the Act were being ramped up, three important Espionage Act cases were prosecuted. These cases involved Charles Schenck in one case, Jacob Frohwerk in another and Eugene Debs in a third. The briefs were written and submitted by Alfred Bettman, special assistant to the Attorney General in charge of prosecution under the Espionage Act.

Schenck was the general secretary of the Socialist Party in Philadelphia and published 15,000 anti-war leaflets. Some leaflets were mailed to men who were subsequently drafted. The pamphlets, among other things, urged the readers to "assert and support your rights" by upholding "democracy." Schenck was arrested, tried and convicted. Justice Oliver Wendell Holmes, after reviewing the content of the leaflet, determined that Schenck would not have printed and circulated the leaflet unless he had intended it to have the effect of causing men to resist the draft, and upheld the conviction. It was in this case that Holmes applied the "clear and present danger" test to speech (Johnson, 1958).

In the space of a single year, Justice Holmes went from a conservative interpretation of "clear and present danger" to a more libertarian interpretation. Thus in the early free speech opinions, he interpreted "clear and present danger" in the context of the common law crime of seditious libel, which turned on any utterance or printed word which criticized the "form, officers, conduct or policies of the government if such criticism could be construed" as painting the government in a bad light or disturbing the peace (Ragan, 1971). In these cases, the question of freedom of speech revolved around the question of "prior restraint," the idea that the government could not and should not stop the printing or distribution of printed material, or the speech of an individual before the act of speaking, but that once the speech act had occurred, the government, as willed by the public, could determine whether the speech was offensive to public sensibility and thus be punished.

The test Justice Holmes was to employ in later cases involved a proximity test, which meant that some type of direct correlation between the speech and incitement to criminal behavior needed to be shown. Much of the free speech debate from the end of 1919 on revolved around the question of the nature and scope of First Amendment protections and what utterances were protected speech and what were considered subject to governmental control during times of national crisis (Ragan, 1971).

Another early Espionage Act case the Supreme Court heard was that of Frohwerk, editor of the Missouri Staats Zeitung. He was charged with writing thirteen anti-war articles published between July and December 1917. The brief Bettman submitted argued that the "main tenor" of the articles was "that Germany committed no wrong against the United States; that this country entered into the war for the benefit of England and the rich men; that the official reasons for our entrance into the war, such as the benefit of democracy and wrongs committed against us by Germany, are mere pretenses" (Ragan, 1971). Justice Oliver Wendell Holmes of the Supreme Court wrote in upholding the Frohwerk conviction that "it is impossible to say that it [the court record] might not have been found that the circulation of the paper was in quarters where a little breath would be enough to kindle a flame" of resistance (Ragan, 1971).

In the Debs case, the conviction was based on a speech that Debs gave on June 16, 1918, in Canton, Ohio. Eugene Debs was well known, having received a million votes in his run as the Socialist Party candidate for President in 1912 (Stone, 2003). In a speech, Debs stated that wars were declared by the "master class" and fought by the "subject class": "The master class has had all to gain and nothing to lose, while the subject class has had nothing to gain and all to lose – especially their lives" (Ragan, 1971). During the speech, Justice Department agents were able to gather evidence that men of draft age were present. The presence of those draft age individuals provided the basis for the government's prosecution of Debs.

In this decision, Justice Holmes determined that Debs' intent could be inferred from the Socialist party's Saint Louis platform opposing the war. Noting that the jury had been instructed not to hate the speech but to determine if the speech was calculated to bring resistance to the draft or the war and Justice Holmes determined that the jury, in convicting Debs, had discharged its duty properly.

The Espionage Act was also used to prosecute people nobody had ever heard of. One of those individuals was Mollie Steimer, a Russian-Jewish émigré who handed out anti-war leaflets in Yiddish on New York's East Side. This stifling of dissent for national security purposes may have been considered necessary for the security of the state at the time.

Some judges who had been against the application of the Espionage Act, started to pen decisions that viewed free speech rights more liberally. Judges Learned Hand in New York and Justice Holmes, as well as Judges George Bourquin and Charles Amidon were among those judges (Stone, 2003).

To remedy this situation, Congress passed the Sedition Act of 1918. This Act made it criminal, among other things, for "any person to utter, print, write, or publish any disloyal, profane, scurrilous, or abusive language intended to cause contempt or scorn for the form of government of the United States, the Constitution, or the flag, or to utter any words supporting the cause of any country at war with the United States or opposing the cause of the United States" (Stone, 2003). In this way, the judges were left with little discretion in attempting to apply First Amendment protection to political speech in the face of the Act.

After the war, the Russian Revolution was determined to be a danger to the United States, and Attorney General A. Mitchell Palmer formed the General Intelligence Division (GID) within the FBI to investigate radicals and radical activities. The GID conducted raids in 33 cities, arresting more than 5,000 on suspicion of radicalism. Attorney General Palmer reported that the "alien filth" the GID had captured were individuals with "sly and crafty eyes... lopsided faces, sloping brows and misshapen features" and that their minds were filled with "cupidity, cruelty... and crime." Over 1,000 of these individuals were summarily deported (Stone, 2003).

Some observers after the war tried to make sense of the question of the right of freedom of speech during wartime. Speaking of the First Amendment, one author wrote, "If the sinews of our political body cannot bear the strain of war, they fail of their fundamental purpose...

If our creed is merely a peace-time panacea, it is wholly unfit to exist. For the world is forever at war" (Garrett, 1919).

In the end, the Red menace was defeated, and in 1920 Congress repealed the Sedition Act.

World War II – The Smith Act and Japanese Detentions

One and a half years before the December 7, 1941 attack on Pearl Harbor and the United States entry into World War II, on June 28, 1940, President Franklin D. Roosevelt signed into law what was commonly known at the time as the Smith Act. The Alien Registration Act of 1940, or Smith Act, had several provisions, including making it illegal for an individual to advocate overthrowing the U.S. government by force or violence, have membership in an organization which advocated such violence, or conspire to overthrow the government. There were only a couple of prosecutions during World War II. The first involved 18 members of the Socialist Workers Party in 1941 and the second, 28 pro-Nazi individuals in 1942. In the second trial, the judge died seven months into the trial and it was never revisited and therefore was dismissed for failure to prosecute (Johnson, 1958).

After the War, in 1949, 11 Communists were convicted under the Act in federal court in New York City of conspiracy to overthrow the government. The Supreme Court sustained the convictions of Dennis and his associates in 1951, and therefore sustained the Act's validity. This decision cleared the way for prosecution of Communists. The government vigorously pursued Communists in order to safeguard the Homeland. By 1956, 131 persons had been indicted, and 98 of those were convicted, 9 acquitted and 24 trials resulted in no verdict by the juries (Johnson, 1958).

In the case of Lawrence Dennis, the Supreme Court upheld the Act because the Act prohibited advocacy, not speech per se. So an academic discussion of Marxism was permitted, but to advocate action against the government was illegal. This finding was in line with the Court's finding in the earlier case, Schenck v. United States. In Schenck, Justice Holmes, in the majority decision, affirmed that if the advocate's speech presented "a clear and present danger" then it was actionable. This rule was then modified to be a rule of "clear and probable" danger in Dennis, and under that legal theory, the rhetorical speech act of Dennis and his associates was actionable under the statute (Johnson, 1958).

The Supreme Court in 1957 heard Yates v. United States, in which the Court narrowed the definition of advocacy and allowed many Communists to escape prosecution. The Court decided that there should be some sufficiency of evidence of anti-government speech before convicting an individual. The fact of Dennis being a leader of the Communist Party was evidentially sufficient to convict back in the late 1940s. The new view of the 1950s Court was that being a leader of an organization dedicated to the overthrow of the United States government was not enough to convict without evidence of the proscribed speech (Johnson, 1958).

On a parallel timeline, on February 19, 1942, President Roosevelt signed Executive Order 9066. This order effectively set up the Japanese internment camps. Neither the words Japanese nor Japanese-American appeared in the order, yet the effect was that in 1942, 120,000 persons of Japanese descent were resettled. Two-thirds of these were American citizens, and the total represented 90% of the total of all Japanese-Americans. In Korematsu v. United States in 1944, the Supreme Court upheld the actions in interring the Japanese Americans in terms of national security. Justice Hugo Black wrote for the majority, "Hardships are part of war, and war is an aggregation of hardships." (Lofgren, 2005).

The Japanese-Americans were released at the end of the war, and those who lived long enough received reparations payments from the government during the Reagan administration (D. Yoo, 1996).

Korean Conflict & Cold War – McCarran-Walters

During the Korean Conflict, the Congress passed the Immigration and Nationality Act of 1952, more popularly known as the McCarran-Walters Act. This Act reformed the immigration laws and created a single referential law for immigration into the country. The Act gave the Attorney General wide discretionary powers on issues of deportation and allowed the Attorney General broad authority in the matter of waiving restrictions on exclusion of aliens whom the Congress may have intended to exclude (Bennett, 1966).

Additionally, there were provisions in the Act which allowed the government to strip citizens of their citizenship for various offenses (Graham, 2005). The Act had provisions for denying visas and expediting the deportation of resident aliens. Chief among these offenses was if in individual was a member of the Communist Party, or if the individual in any way helped enemies of the United States with money or other aid (Margolick, 1982).

In 1954, Congress passed the Communist Control Act. This Act outlawed the Communist Party. Other measures were also put in place for the national security – including extensive loyalty programs and infiltration of subversive organizations (Marx, 1974; Goldstein, 2006). It was also during this time that the House Un-American Activities Committee investigated various individuals' political affiliations (Carr, 1951).

The Vietnam Conflict

The Vietnam War era brought nothing new in terms of legislation to limit personal freedom. The state determined that the main dangers to the established order (the Establishment) at that time were the civil rights and anti-war movements. The groups were infiltrated and put under surveillance through undercover work.

J. Edgar Hoover launched COINTELPRO in 1956, and the FBI operated against dissident groups – and encompassed operations against socialist, white hate, black nationalist, civil rights, anti-war and New Left groups. These operations were able to achieve their objectives until 1976, when the Senate moved to limit domestic security activities (Garrow, 1988).

The USA PATRIOT Act

September 11 precipitated the passage of the Uniting and Strengthening America by Providing Appropriate Tools Required to Intercept and Obstruct Terrorism (USA PATRIOT) Act of 2001. The Act was signed into law on October 26, 2001. There were some sunset provisions in the

Act as a protection for civil liberties. The Act has subsequently been renewed, with revisions and expansion of the government's powers. Many of the sunset provisions were nullified by the extension and expansion of provisions of the Act with the signing of H.R. 2417 "Intelligence Authorization Act for Fiscal Year 2004" (G. Bush, 2003) on December 13, 2003, H.R. 3199 "USA PATRIOT Improvement and Reauthorization Act of 2005" on March 13, 2006, and S 2271 "USA PATRIOT Act Additional Reauthorizing Amendments Act of 2006" on the same day (G. Bush, 2006). (The reference is correct, on the White House Web site, the title was as it is printed here).

The PATRIOT Act grants intelligence agencies the ability to monitor communications, conduct searches of United States citizens' residences without informing the target of the search, and gather any manner of information from third parties without any judicial oversight. This means that searches can be conducted without the issue of a warrant based on probable cause (Jordan, 2007) and is therefore a complete abridgement of the Fourth Amendment.

The vehicle of choice for seizure of all types of records is the issue of a National Security Letter (NSL). The NSL allows the FBI to go to a business and obtain any information for which the FBI asks. No judge is required for the issuance of a NSL. There are some guidelines. Additionally, in "emergency" situations, the FBI is allowed to seize information using an "exigent letter." These exigent letters are also only to be issued after some type of procedure is followed (Jordan, 2007).

An audit by the Justice Department Inspector General Glenn A. Fine uncovered irregularities in the FBI's following of its own procedures for issuing National Security Letters. The FBI underreported the number of letters issued by 22%, some letters were used for improper purposes, exigent letters were issued without proper authorization, and according to the FBI's own count, at least 26 instances of the issue of NSLs were in violation of the procedures the FBI itself enumerated (Jordan, 2007).

The PATRIOT Act authorizes intelligence and domestic surveillance agencies to turn over the information gathered without probable cause to prosecutors. The prosecutors can then use the evidence in the prosecution of ordinary criminal cases. The custodians of the records who surrendered those records are prohibited from informing anyone (especially the target of what in the past would have been an illegal search) that they surrendered those records (Dunham, 2005)

The PATRIOT Act received a boost on December 13, 2003, with the signing into law of the Intelligence Authorization Act for Fiscal Year 2004. As Andrew Napolitano wrote on March 5, 2004, for the Wall Street Journal:

> This statute expands the term "financial institution" so as to include travel agencies and car dealers, casinos and hotels, real estate and insurance agents and lawyers, newsstands and pawn brokers, and even the Post Office. (para. 4)

When these powers are used against U.S. citizens in cases which do not involve national security, the Constitution's Fourth Amendment guarantees against unreasonable searches have been circumvented, in that no warrant is issued. No judge must determine if there is probable cause. In the past, a search required a search warrant specifying the place to be searched and the thing to be seized.

To illustrate the scope of the powers the government was interested in granting to itself, one needs only look at the events of early 2003 in the quest to pass the next generation, i.e. post-PATRIOT Act, surveillance law.

In January 2003 the Justice Department created "The Domestic Security Enhancement Act" which was sent to selected Congressmen on the Hill, but not to the full Congress at the time. A Congressional staffer had leaked the document to the press. When asked about the leaked document, a Justice Department spokesman, Mark Corallo, told the Village Voice that the legislation would be "filling in the holes" in the original PATRIOT Act, and would be "refining things that will enable us to do our job." The circulation of the draft with proposals for over 100 new provisions was attributed to Attorney General John Ashcroft (Welch, 2003).

The public debate and controversy which ensued resulted in some setbacks in expanding the powers of the USA PATRIOT Act. At the time, Attorney General Ashcroft "denied a bill was in the works, although he admitted that the leaked document is 'what we've been thinking'" ("EFF Analysis," n.d.).

One of the features the draft Domestic Security and Enhancement Act would have indemnified law enforcement and intelligence officials from being prosecuted for violating federal law when conducting these warrantless wiretaps or illegal searches as long as the officers were only following orders. Subsequent to the leak regarding the President's authorization of warrantless wiretaps by the NSA in late 2001, observers reached the conclusion that the draft legislation leaked in 2003 was an attempt to legalize the NSA warrantless wiretapping program (Welch, 2003).

The Administration later claimed that the draft legislation leaked in January 2003 was not the legislation that the Administration wanted. According to Justice Department spokesperson Tasia Scolinos, "These proposals were drafted by junior staffers and never formally presented to the attorney general or the White House. They were not drafted with the NSA program in mind." (Eggen, 2006)

CHAPTER 2:

Foundational Theory of Surveillance

The reason given for the types of surveillance that the government conducts against American citizens involves the desire to avert another terrorist attack such as 9/11. According to former Attorney General John Ashcroft, President Bush told him, "Don't ever let this happen again" (D. Solomon, 2006)

The advocates of the total surveillance regime that the U.S. government is in the process of imposing on the population of the United States argue that there is a logically straight line from the destruction of personal privacy protections under the Constitution to the prevention of terrorism. Conversely, it can be stated that the manner in which terrorism can be best prevented is to put every person under surveillance. The analogy is made by one of John Poindexter's associates, Ted Senator:

> Our task is akin to finding dangerous groups of needles hidden in stacks of needle pieces. This is much harder than simply finding needles in a haystack: we have to search through many stacks, not just one; we do not have a contrast between shiny, hard needles and dull, fragile hay; we have many ways of putting the pieces together into individual needles and the needles into groups of needles; and we cannot tell if a needle or group is dangerous until it is at least partially assembled. So, in principle at least, we must track all the needle pieces all of the time and consider all possible combinations (Bamford, 2008, p. 102).

John Poindexter was the driving force behind Total Information Awareness (TIA), the program started under the aegis of the Department of Defense. Poindexter graduated at the top of his class at the Naval Academy, but was also the highest ranking official to be found guilty as a result of his role in the Iran-Contra scandal (Bamford, 2008). TIA was the method the government was going to use to track the needles and try to assemble all of the combinations that the needle pieces could make.

Most of the literature which advances surveillance as a solution to terrorism and/or defends the practice of surveillance advances (or defends) the theory that increased surveillance decreases terrorism and/or crime. This theory is advanced without a evidence; the assertion is made as an article of faith. It is argued that surveillance as a preventive measure is a postulate that needs no explanation. Examples are proffered of the practical effects of surveillance (*Report From the Field*, 2004) Statements are made to the effect that the surveillance works.. But again, these statements must be taken on faith because the public is told that they cannot learn the manner in which it works (Levey, 2006) because to do so would compromise the effect of it working.

The theory of surveillance as a tool to prevent terrorism appears to have two components. The first component involves finding and tracking known terrorists. Once a terrorist is found, the tracking is not stopped nor the terrorist apprehended. The next phase involves finding the wider the web of relationships of which the terrorist is part. The web of investigation grows, and the people associated with the initial individual being investigated, are themselves investigated, and then their associates. Of course, there is the argument that, this being the case, bin Laden should have been caught by now (Devita-Raeburn, 2008).

Devita-Raeburn examined Stanley Milgram's original small world study (Milgram, 1967). Even though Devita-Raeburn noted weaknesses in the statistical analysis of the study, the supposition that a web of connections will lead to any specific individual is ingrained in the culture. In Milgram's study, some of the chains connecting people could be explained by observing the socio-economic status of the subjects and their motivation, in that the chains that were not completed due to some connectivity failure, failed to complete because of a lack of motivation. Additionally, the original Milgram study used and targeted individuals in average to above-average socio-economic classes which tended to have more connections among more strata.

Milgram (1974) was also famous for his study of obedience in which experimental subjects were tested to see at what point they would stop administering painful electric shocks to actors posing as experimental subjects. In a shocking reprise of circumstances thought to be similar to those that Nazi camp guards and soldiers would encounter, almost all of the subjects in Milgram's famous experiment were to administer what they believed were fatal doses of electric current (Milgram, 1974). It is useful to bear in mind that in the Milgram study, law-abiding citizens conducted themselves in unlawful ways based on the assurance that what they did was necessary. Thus, when members of the security apparatus in today's society are asked to break the law, such as in the case of warrantless wiretapping activities, or when issuing National Security Letters in violation of FBI guidelines (Jordan, 2007), for the "security of the country," it is easy to understand that they may be well-intentioned but misinformed and misguided criminals.

The second component involves monitoring individuals' activities and using the results of this monitoring to predict whether the individual is going to commit a terrorist act. In the immediate circumstance, the individual's behavior would be compared with the behavior of an individual who was about to commit a terrorist act. The baseline for prediction would be developed by monitoring everyone all the time, then when someone commits a terrorist act, the activities of that individual could be replayed up to the point of the launch of the attack. The theory is that if the behavior of the newly observed individual matches the behavior of those who have launched terrorist attacks in the past, prior to the launch of the attack, then the individual exhibiting that behavior could be prevented from committing the terrorist attack. This thinking was behind the other purpose of the Total Information Awareness (TIA) program.

There are now only gross approximations of indicators that law enforcement and intelligence community members use to identify potential terrorists (leaving out the rhetorical question of who would not be a "potential terrorist"), and some of these are bad for journalists. For instance, according to the current law enforcement manuals, the use of cameras and video equipment is considered to be a precursor to terrorism (Goodman, Rosa, German, & Clancy, 2008)

It is instructive to understand the rationale of the surveillance advocates and attempt to find the reasons behind society's redefinition of the right of privacy. The rhetoric of surveillance proponents is a good place to start and can be examined in the context of post 9/11 legal and policy initiatives knowing that there had been significant work in the surveillance arena prior to the attacks of 9/11, on both the pro and con sides of the issue. This rhetoric must be examined in the light of the terrorist threat which underpins the reasons that citizens seem unconcerned for their liberty. There has been an attitude based in fear of terror that citizens should trust the government to use the powers it has gained by circumventing the Constitution for society's benefit.

What is Terrorism?

Various government agencies and recognized experts in the field of terrorism have constructed and apply differing definitions of the term "terrorism." In popular discourse, unpopular individuals and causes are labeled terrorists (Pabst, 2006). The term as used in the press is amorphous and is commonly misapplied by media and government interests (Pumphrey, 2003). Before September 11, 2001, however, there were attempts to define terrorism in ways in which scholars could agree. After September 11, the definition of "terrorism" has been drawn so broadly as to include almost anyone the system desires to include.

The serious attempts in the field of terrorism studies to define the term terrorism have led to various degrees of precision in defining the term. Badey (1999) attempts to define terrorism while noting that "there is still no commonly accepted definition of international terrorism" (p.90). Badey refers to work by Alex P. Schmid, attempting to craft a definition of terrorism as a synthesis of 109 definitions. The result was a very precise, yet very verbose definition. Badey contrasts the Schmid definition with the 1983 definition contained in Title 22 of the United States Code, Section 2656(d), which is shorter, yet more general. Badey correctly notes that governments define terrorism in ways that allow them maximum flexibility in characterizing politically significant events in terms advantageous to the government describing those events.

Pragmatically, due to the multi-national nature of terrorism, it seems as if it would be important for states to agree on the definition of terrorism in order to cooperate in the suppression of terrorism, although states are generally in agreement with what constitutes terrorism in times of peace. The definition has evolved in the rubric of "customary law" over time (Cassese, 2006). However, in other circumstances, such as in terms of armed resistance to an occupation, there is less agreement. There is an element of one political or policy interest group's "terrorist" as another's "freedom fighter." Under international law, there are distinctions between violations regarding civilian populations for states – such that states can rarely be held accountable for "state-sponsored terrorism." (Cassese, 2006) The key to avoiding violating international law is for the state to kill (or at least attack) an "enemy combatant" and keep the incidence of civilian deaths (collateral damage) from being "disproportionate." The big disagreement is what to do with "freedom fighters" who are fighting to end an occupation, and what their culpability is in the case of civilian casualties. In almost every case, it is agreed that non-state actors killing civilians are guilty of terrorism, while killing civilians in an armed conflict could, in the worst case for the state as aggressor, raise the offense to only the status of "war crime." (Cassese, 2006)

Hoffman (1998) also looked at 109 definitions of terrorism and calculated the frequencies of certain conceptual elements, including violence, that terrorism is political, emphasis on fear etc. Broad variations in frequency were found, with (only) 83.5% of the definitions including violence or force conceptually, to the idea of demands being made on third parties included in only four percent of the definitions (Hoffman, 1998). Thus there is a wide variation in the intersection of definitional elements, allowing for rhetors to manipulate the meaning of what is considered to be terrorism by merely choosing the definition of terrorism.

The term terror entered the lexicon originating from a description of state action during the French Revolution. The Terrors were a tool of the state to enforce compliance and order during the period of turmoil following the uprisings of 1789, specifically the French government's actions against their domestic enemies in 1793 and 1794 (Tilly, 2004). Therefore, the use of the term terror in a political context in the modern day is well-divorced from the manner of use of the term from the time of the French Revolution.

Terrorism, according to the United States Department of State in 1983, was explicitly described as political and a tool used by non-state actors or "clandestine agents." This was the manner in which modern international terrorism was presented in the popular discourse prior to 9/11. Acts of terror in definitions of terrorism are designed to induce fear which would influence behavior. Many definitions are concerned with the repeatability of acts of terror. If an act in itself is an isolated act of terror which has no possibility of being repeated, is it terrorism under the definition? (Badey, 1998) In the popular discourse, the Oklahoma City bombing, even though it had no possibility of being repeatable (by the same perpetrator(s) or organization, as the government said there was no organization), is referred to as terrorism (Lewis, 2000).

Historically, modern terror's origins can be traced to the Narodnaya Volva (People's Will) in czarist Russia. The group was founded in 1878 with the purpose of committing dramatic acts of violence to awaken the apathetic Russian people and rally them to the anti-czarist cause. There was a successful assassination, that of Czar in 1881.

Operationally, the chain of events following the assassination led to anarchists and anti-government revolutionaries discovering the concept of organizing into small "cells", or groups of individuals. This organization into cells served the purposes of avoiding detection by police and minimizing the amount of damage to which discovery could lead if one of the members would be discovered and confess their anti-government associations (Hoffman, 1998).

Anarchists were responsible for several political assassinations, including the assassination of Archduke Franz Ferdinand in Sarajevo in 1914. Despite their success in killing heads of state and politically important personages, those events did not have the effects desired by the revolutionists. Political life and power structures were not changed by these events.

Anarchists were described as such during that historical period, although their actions could arguably fit into the definition of terrorism. Their actions were repeatable, in that they were attempting to build an international fellowship of anarchists. Their aim was to affect behavior, hoping to affect political change in all spheres of political and societal structure. Their actions were intended to affect the target group, in this case individuals in power, and there was a certain amount of fear that they hoped to inspire in the target groups (Hoffman, 1998). Thus, anarchists could be considered ideologically motivated terrorists.

States are also known to sponsor terrorists for their political ends. These terrorists are known as "state-sponsored terrorists." These terrorists are considered to be even more dangerous than terrorists who must raise their own money. State-sponsored terrorists have access to money and expertise to which they would not otherwise have access. The danger that state-sponsored terrorists pose to their "constituents" is that state-sponsored terrorists also have latitude to conduct operations that they might not have contemplated were they not sponsored; operations which might cause collateral damage among their perceived constituents, due to the disconnect between their funding sources and the actual population they are ostensibly representing (Jenkins, 1986).

The destructive capability of terrorist groups at all times throughout history was limited by the capabilities of the weapons they could bring under their control. These weapons, by definition, were the most deadly weapons existent at the time. Prior to the advent of gunpowder, terrorists would have had to use knives and swords. With gunpowder, there was the ability to make bombs. Until the advent of weapons of mass destruction, the best terrorists could do was to use explosives. With the use and availability of chemical, biological and nuclear weapons came the ability to cause damage on a much greater scale than at any previous time in history (Laqueur, 1999).

These more powerful and more destructive weapons also require a will to use them. Laqueur (1999) describes the "New Terrorism," which involves terrorists who have the will to use weapons of great destructive power. The motivations of these terrorists may not traditional in the sense that they are working toward what would be considered politically achievable aims. The motivations that these terrorists possess are expected to be extreme, and possibly the most dangerous, extreme position is that of religious fanaticism.

The Terrorist Threat

The United States government asserts that the reason the government is compelled to conduct surveillance on its citizens is that the government must protect the citizens of the country from terrorism. The claim is that surveillance is necessary to discover and pre-empt terrorists. The seminal event which the government points to in generating consensus for its surveillance activities is the attack of September 11, 2001 (Bloss, 2008). Terrorism studies scholars have attempted to rigorously define the meaning of the term "terrorism." The term terrorism is used differently in popular discourse than the manner in which scholars use the term. This observation is included due to the fact that it is the popular definition of terrorism which is used in justifying policy decisions made by the government and to obtain consent for those decisions (Badey, 1998; "USA Patriot Act," 2001).

The U.S. government's official story for the events of 9/11 is that 19 men, 15 individuals from Saudi Arabia, two individuals from the United Arab Emirates, one from Egypt and one from Lebanon were involved in the hijackings and subsequent crashing of airplanes into the World Trade Center and the Pentagon on September 11, 2001 (Johnston, 2003). Department of Homeland Security Michael Chertoff referred to the attacks of 9/11 as a defining moment in U.S. history (Chertoff, 2006a).

September of 2001 was not, however, the first time that the World Trade Center had been attacked. A truck with a bomb in it had been driven into the parking garage in 1993 and detonated, leaving six dead and over 1,000 wounded ("Significant Terrorist Incidents," 2004). Similarly, according to the State Department, the bombing in Oklahoma City, a single incident attributed to Terry Nichols and Timothy McVeigh, is considered terrorism ("Significant Terrorist Incidents," 2004). Although the Oklahoma City bombing lacked repeatability, which most scholarship considers to be a litmus test in the definition of terror (Badey, 1998; Hoffman, 1998), under the PATRIOT Act, passed in October 2001, the Oklahoma City bombing is definitely considered to be terrorism. Under many definitions of terrorism, a pattern of lighting churches on fire or bombing abortion clinics could be considered domestic terrorism.

The USA Patriot Act in Section 802, expanded the definition of domestic terrorism for criminal consideration to include "...activities that— (A) involve acts dangerous to human life that are a violation of the criminal laws of the United States or of any State; (B) appear to be intended— (i) to intimidate or coerce a civilian population; (ii) to influence the policy of a government by intimidation or coercion; or (iii) to affect the conduct of a government by mass destruction, assassination, or kidnapping; and (C) occur primarily within the territorial jurisdiction of the United States" ("USA Patriot Act," 2001).

Pre-empting Terrorists

There are several components to the art or science of preventing terrorism. Identifying terrorists would seem to be the first thing to do. Intuitively, the first thought would be to identify and apprehend those who have committed terrorist acts in the past, and punish them.

However, according to surveillance theory as practiced by the United States government, it appears the idea would be to observe and monitor the terrorists and allow the known terrorists to lead investigators to additional terrorists. The theory involves the supposition that those who may have committed terrorist acts in the past would associate with those who would commit terrorist acts in the future with a higher probability and frequency than the average United States citizen.

The 9/11 Commission investigated the sequence of events that led to the attacks on September 11, 2001. Commission investigators pieced together a picture of who knew what and when. The 9/11 report indicates that the government had knowledge of the identities and whereabouts of key terrorists involved in the 9/11 hijackings, and despite ample warning that these individuals were in the United States, did nothing to stop them (9/11_Commission, 2004). Additionally and after the fact, (Bamford, 2008), in interviews conducted at NSA, discovered that no 9/11 Commission members interviewed anyone from NSA to see what was known at that agency. It turns out that NSA knew the terrorists were interesting targets and was listening in on the 9/11 hijackers for months before the attacks. NSA passed the information to CIA and the information was then not forwarded to the

FBI for investigation. It is accepted as fact that there were key failures in the handoff of information regarding these terrorists (9/11_Commission, 2004). This highlights an important problem in the growing surveillance society: there is so much information potentially and actually available that interagency communication and prioritization is problematic. In theory, security agencies suffer from information overload.

Two of the alleged hijackers, Nawaf al-Hazni and Khalid al-Mihdhar, were known to the U.S. intelligence community for their involvement with the 1998 embassy bombings in Tanzania and Kenya. It is accepted that these bombings had been the work of al-Qaeda, and these al-Hazni and Mihdar were implicated as perpetrators. In January 2000, it was discovered that these two individuals were in attendance at a secret terrorist planning meeting in Kuala Lumpur. In March 2000, the CIA had been informed of the fact that al-Hazmi flew to Los Angeles from Malaysia on United Airlines. The CIA failed to notify any agency which could have stopped or monitored al-Hazmi. Denying entry to the U.S., arrest or surveillance against al-Hazmi was possible under the laws as they existed at the time (Jonas & Harper, 2006).

NSA director, General Mike Hayden, had been worried about getting the NSA in trouble for breaking the law, as the agency had been in trouble for breaking the law prior to 2001. Therefore, the director in 2001, even though his agency had been intercepting those known terrorists' communication, did not divulge information gleaned from the surveillance. General Hayden stopped monitoring all calls involving any person in the U.S., including calls of suspected terrorists (Bamford, 2008).

Before the meeting in Kuala Lumpur, the NSA had intercepted a call placed to Khalid al-Mindhar in late December 1999. This intercepted call terminated at a house in Yemen the intelligence community knew al-Qaeda was using as an operations center. The base of operations had been used in planning the operation against the U.S.S. Cole and was identified as such in the investigation into the attack on the Cole. The NSA only picked up first names in the call indicating that the terrorists would be meeting in Kuala Lumpur. The failure by the NSA to look up the names Khalid and Nawaf was the first of many failures of the intelligence community. In the case of this first NSA failure, it is reported that the NSA was deliberately doing as little as possible in identifying the subjects of their investigation due to rivalries with the CIA (Bamford, 2008).

If the goal of surveillance is anti-terrorism and the identification of terrorists, the apprehension of terrorists would be doable without the new powers the government has granted itself. The logical conclusion is that the surveillance regime, as it was constituted before the current push for ubiquitous surveillance, if correctly applied, would have resulted in the apprehension of the individuals who posed a threat to the United States. The government had all the information it needed to prevent the attacks of 9/11 with the intelligence apparatus it possessed at the time. The question becomes one of what is to be gained in an anti-terrorsism sense by new incursions against American citizens' individual privacy—certainly much stands to be lost.

Another component involves the idea that once these terrorists are identified, their associates could also be identified, on the theory that those individuals with which the terrorists are in communication would be individuals who might pose a risk to the United States. In this case, terrorists would be identified, surveilled, and then their associates would be identified and surveilled. If it were a case-by-case paradigm, which terrorism investigations were under the pre-PATRIOT Act paradigm, at some point one would expect that the terrorists would be picked up and prosecuted, and the surveillance would then cease.

A corollary to this theory of surveilling terrorists involves the placement of terrorists and their known associates' names on various lists. Some of the lists include the No-Fly List and the Terrorist Watch List (Goodman et al., 2008). The theory behind keeping lists holds that a terrorist might not know he/she has been identified as a terrorist, and would attempt to board a plane or enter through a border checkpoint, use a real name, and be apprehended. As of October 2010, unfortunately for the proponents of this theory, there have been no known instances of a terrorist being apprehended in this manner. There are many instances, however, of people who have been harassed and delayed in their attempts to fly. Some of these included Catherine Stevens, wife of Senator Ted Stevens (R-Alaska) and Senator Ted Kennedy (D-Massachusetts). In Catherine Stevens' case, her name is similar to the name of a formerly popular rock and roll singer whose stage name was Cat Stevens but who now goes by the name of Yusuf Islam. Ted Kennedy had been repeatedly delayed because there was supposedly an Irish terrorist who had gone by that name (Marek, 2007). The theory of list-keeping's proponents is the hope that at some point a terrorist will fall into the No-Fly List trap that the government has set.

Alternatively, the government might actually keep the list as a mechanism to scare terrorists away from airplanes. This would tend to keep them from being able to travel freely in the U.S., tripping tracking mechanisms when they show up at airports. This also assumes that even with all of the new surveillance powers the government has that somehow the terrorists are lost in the shuffle until they show up at the airport, thus alerting the government as to their whereabouts.

The most overarching view of terrorism, its prevention, and the surveillance necessary to achieve this preventative stance can be found in the rhetoric of the government's political appointees who are responsible for evangelizing for the need for total surveillance. Part of this surveillance involves the warrantless wiretapping program and other data collection efforts by the NSA. In addition to digitizing and recording everyone's phone calls, the NSA has been recording and examining credit card transactions, banking transaction, Internet searches and flight bookings... everything that people do that leaves any type of electronic trail. Although not explicitly stated, one would assume that this "transactional" data includes geo-location data, therefore tracking everyone's movements also. Gorman explicitly states that the geo-location of the cell phones at the time of the call is stored, but does not address the question of geo-location data associated with just walking around without being on the phone. (Gorman, 2008)

John Yoo has been responsible for some of the current thought on the manner in which terrorists can be preempted. In his explanation for the reasons that the President has the authorization to order surveillance without having to follow procedures that would normally have to be followed under FISA, the operational advantages of illegal surveillance are extolled. General Hayden, director of the NSA during the warrantless wiretapping program, said that the program had been successful in detecting and preventing attacks in the United States but of course could not elaborate. The American people have to take his word for it. Attorney General Alberto Gonzalez also stated that the programs had been effective (J. Yoo, 2006, p. 104).

According to GWOT U.S. government thinking, the most dangerous terrorist organization is al Qaeda. Al Qaeda is held as responsible for 9/11, the attack on the U.S.S. Cole, and bombings at two embassies in Africa, among other attacks. Therefore, the government is very concerned with members of al Qaeda's movements and intentions.

Religious Extremists and Their Effect on Geopolitics

Al Qaeda is an organization of terrorists with the stated goal of attacking the West. These terrorists are motivated by religion as an ideology. The terrorists who are members of this organization are also fanatics to the point of being able to commit suicide in the course of their terrorism (Doran, 2002).

On September 11, 2001, United Airlines Flight 175 struck the South Tower of the World Trade Center. American Airlines Flight 11 crashed into the North Tower of the World Trade Center. American Airlines Flight 77 flew into the Pentagon. United Airlines Flight 93 did not make it to its intended target. The passengers, having been alerted to the other hijacking events, overpowered the hijackers and the United Flight 93 crashed into a field in Pennsylvania. It was speculated that United 93 was heading toward the Capitol or the White House (9/11_Commission, 2004).

The latest official count of the people who died in the World Trade Center on 9/11 is 2751. The total number of people died in the attacks that day was 2975 ("Official 9/11 Death Toll," 2008), and the American public was horrified.

Prior to September 11, al-Qaeda had attacked several other Western targets with varying degrees of success. In August 1998, two American embassies were bombed simultaneously. At the embassy in Nairobi, Kenya, the bombing killed 12 Americans, 32 other United States employees, and over 200 Kenyans. In Dar es Salaam, Tanzania, no Americans were killed, however 11 individuals were killed and 85 injured (Crenshaw, 2001). In October 2000, the U.S.S. Cole was attacked by a boat retrofitted as a bomb, 17 American servicemen were killed, and 39 were injured (Abdul-Alim, 2000).

At that time, Al Qaeda was becoming a powerful terrorist network, capable of international terrorism on a scale that was of concern to the United States. After the embassy bombings, the United States retaliated with cruise missile strikes against al Qaeda training camps in Afghanistan, and a pharmaceutical plant in Sudan (Crenshaw, 2001).

Al-Qaeda also has a pre-history which is sometimes overlooked. Starting with the Carter administration, agencies of the United States government gave financial support and arms to the mujahedeen to fight the Soviet Union in Afghanistan (Schneider & Schneider, 2002).

There is disagreement over the structure of al Qaeda, whether it is a coherent international terror organization, or merely a loose, informal affiliation of like-minded terrorist operatives (Burke, 2004). Rohan Gunartana in hearings before a United States Congressional committee stated that al Qaeda was organized according to a charter published in Al Jihad, a publication printed in Peshawar, Pakistan in March 1988 (*Terrorism, Al Qaed*, 2003). Mr. Gunartana quotes the publication as claiming that "al Qaeda is the vanguard, 'the pioneering vanguard of the Islamic movements.'" This vanguard, according to Mr. Gunartana, would inspire other Islamic movements to also attack Western interests.

This manifesto was attributed to Dr. Abdullah Azzam. By the same token, Burke quotes Dr. Azzam as calling in 1987 for al-qaeda al-sulbah, "a vanguard of the strong." These are identical quotations, but are interpreted differently by the two scholars. Burke makes the assertion that the term "al Qaeda" was coined after the 1998 U.S. Embassy bombings in East Africa, in order that American laws could be applied to the perpetrators of those bombings. Burke explains that in 2004, Israeli intelligence services would refer to the Muslim extremists as "jihadi international" instead of "al Qaeda" for the reason that Israeli intelligence considered the jihadi movement to be decentralized and to not have coherent leadership (Burke, 2004).

The amorphous nature of the terminological and definitional semantics makes President Bush's discussion of "al Qaeda in Iraq" either logical or disingenuous, depending on who is listening. Due to the fact that al Qaeda is a distributed organization, with semiautonomous operational units, the order of priorities of the aims of the various al-Qaeda franchises likewise are not necessarily coherent.

Marc Sageman explained to Congress that bin Laden has been crucial in operationally defining the direction and subject of the attacks of these affiliated groups. It was bin Laden's fatwa in 1996 which changed the focus from the "near enemy" to the "far enemy." This involves the concept of corrupted states. As an example, Muslim extremists had been at war with their own government in Egypt. The government of Egypt was considered to be jahiliyya. Jahiliyya refers to the barbaric state of ignorance which existed before the prophet's revelations. Once the Prophet imparted the knowledge contained in the Quran, Islamic states would need to, according to the Salafists, impose Sharia law to be a proper Muslim state (*Terrorism, Al Qaeda*, 2003).

The 9/11 discussion had as its initial focus the terror network headed by Osama Bin Laden. Yet, it was with the help of the Taliban that bin Laden's network was able to flourish and train (*Terrorism, Al Qaeda*, 2003).

Mamoun Fandy, testifying to Congress, made the observation that there were other Islamic terror groups which were coordinating with each other to carry out attacks internationally. The attacks occurred over a wide swath of territories, with multiple countries of origin.

In some scholarly efforts to try to understand the structure and characteristics of terrorist organizations, comparisons have been made between al Qaeda and the Sicilian mafia and pirates of the 17th century. Structurally and functionally, these organizations are similar, even if their motivations are not. For instance they:

> ...have some attributes in common: their cellular and networked structures extending across national boundaries; their high levels of energy, fed by sentiments of revenge; their sponsorship by states or elements of states; their parasitic revenue streams from licit and illicit commerce, and their tendency toward extraordinary violence in some historical moments, provoking a determined, and generally publicly supported, "crackdown." (Schneider & Schneider, 2002, p. 776)

This would then be a hook for the counter-terrorists to take a page out of the book of enforcement efforts used against the mafia. To move against the organizational structure of organizations such as these would entail the types of signals intelligence at which the United States is proficient; intercepted communications, wiretaps and surveillance. Additionally, in mafia cases there would always have been an informant of some type, or some testimony from the inside. In the case of al-Qaeda, there wouldn't seem to be much need for testimony, just location and organizational information as assassination is the preferred method of justice.

Other scholarship involves an attempt to ascribe and understand some type of root cause of Islamic terrorism. One of the common themes has to do with the concerns of anti-globalist sentiment. Market capitalism has transformed the world. Economic historians have identified two main types of exchange, those based on markets and those based on clientalist exchange. Market capitalist transactions are based on contracts.

Markets and market forces are well known to Westerners, as that is the economic system to which the United States and the global trading community adhere. Clientalist structures are mostly recognized as tribal or clan-centric. The members of the community are clients of the tribal leader or head of the clan. These structures manifest themselves as kingdoms or caliphates at the nation-state level of organization, and thus are thought by Western standards to be almost medieval or feudal in nature.

There is a difference in organization of the communities based on these types of systems, wherein clientalist communities are hierarchically organized. All societies have some combination of market and clientalistic characteristics, however the liberal democracies have advanced market-based economies, and few states have predominantly clientalist economies, so this fact might be a key difference in the cultural differences which might lead to feelings of ill-will.

As Mousseau (2002/2003) notes, the in-groups in clientalist societies with mineral wealth can spread that wealth around to maintain and gain more loyalty and to keep power. For societies without mineral wealth, underdevelopment and economic displacement results in increasing the social and civil ills. The market economy appears to be a Western or American invention and therefore the resentment inherent in the society at the economic and social ills is projected on the Western market system and the West in general (Mousseau, 2002/2003).

The United States government is focused on the language of war in the discussion of the "Global War on Terror." From a counter-terrorism perspective it is this rhetoric of war and concern for operational security which makes U.S. intelligence services obsessed with signals intelligence.

Technologies of Surveillance

The types and amount of surveillance an individual may be subject to on a daily basis varies depending on the types of activities in which the individual engages. The technologies of surveillance include Internet and email surveillance, telephone and cell phone surveillance, and video surveillance of public spaces.

The technologies can be divided into content-based and location-based monitoring. That is, the Internet and any kind of phone (used only as phones and not as a location beacon) are of little use for monitoring an individual without the content which is transmitted across the network. If someone is moving around and not talking on the phone or using the Internet, how would those conducting the surveillance know where the individual might be?

The technology of location tracking is demonstrated by the location-assisting technology in cell phones and the monitoring that cameras provide. These technologies present problems in that they are not 100% reliable in tracking individuals. Not everyone has a cell phone. For those who do, even though cell phone tracking takes a fair amount of processing power for triangulation, the exercise of tracking that individual, and all individuals with cell phones, is trivial. Those who own cell phones generally keep their cell phones on or about their persons ("The Cell Phone Challenge," 2006), so tracking them using these beacons is a simple matter.

To achieve universal tracking of individuals, those doing the tracking need some type of mechanism such that every individual has some type of beacon. Ubiquitous RFID tracking fulfills that need. Anything can be tagged and tracked. Tracking is easy enough that even home users can do it (Cangeloso, 2008).

The most unobtrusive tracking technology, and easiest to use for tracking any manner of object is the RFID tag. Advances in technology have produced RFID tags which can be as small as a grain of sand, and therefore can be embedded in almost any item. The component which renders the discovery of RFID tags unobtrusive is the fact that there is no way for the average individual to know that a reader was scanning all of the RFID tags embedded in the items they were wearing or carrying (Fishkin, Jiang, Philipose, & Roy, 2004).

Proponents of RFID espouse a vision of the future in which every discrete item is tagged. Every aspirin bottle, every shoe, every tire, every car, every belt and every pair of jeans would have an RFID chip embedded. Every pair of eyeglasses, purse, backpack, book, pen, pencil, pencil sharpener, package of gum or breath mints; all of these would be tagged. In this future, when an individual walks into a retail establishment, the readers at the doorway would enable the sales staff to know every item that is in an individual's wallet, every item they are wearing and every item they are carrying. With proper data integration, the salesman at the clothes store could tell the customer that his socks were bought several years ago and would the customer like some socks with their purchase ("RFID," 2007).

Under the provisions of law regarding data collection and sharing, every encounter with the reader could legally be written to a national security database under the privacy laws as they stand now. No change to the law would be required to allow this. This would allow the trail of a person shopping at the mall, for instance, to be followed, in real time if necessary. In this way, the government would be able to track every person, and know, for instance, if a person stopped into a book store, did or did not buy something and then went to the clothes store. The few minutes spent looking at the latest gadgets at Radio Shack would be noted, as well as a stop at the information kiosk to ask directions.

With advancements in technology, there could be readers at multiple locations in stores. These arrays of multiple readers would allow those who were watching to know near which products the consumer stopped or loitered. According to experiments which were conducted by International Business Machines (IBM) in Germany, the watchers would know what products were more interesting to consumers, by combining the RFID tracking with feeds from closed circuit television (CCTV) cameras ("German Consumers," 2004). The idea is to determine the time a consumer spends looking at some item by combining the feed from the RFID readers with some other surveillance technologies to help the retailers ("METRO Group," 2008; "Metro opens high-tech shop," 2003).

Sometimes, the surveillance works but is not effectively coordinated with the agencies that need to receive and act on the information. An example of this might be when the United States Agency for International Development (USAID) gives U.S. taxpayer money to individuals and groups tied to terrorists. USAID gave $1 million to an individual with ties to a disciple of bin Laden, and $180,000 to a Bosnian group whose president is on a watch list and is barred from entering the United States (Tankersley, 2007).

CHAPTER 3:

Total Surveillance

Counter-Terrorism

The reason given to the American people for the imposition of dramatic new surveillance measures and the limitation of individuals' rights under the law was the need to fight terrorism. The fundamental assumption is that there is not just a way to discover known and active terrorists through surveillance, but also a way to predict who might become a terrorist and how or when terrorist acts might be committed.

There are two components inherent in the problem of counter-terrorism. The first is to identify terrorists. The second is the question of what to do with the terrorists once they've been identified.

The problem of identifying terrorists can itself be broken down into two elements. The first element is identification of those who have committed terrorist acts in the past. It can further be assumed that those who have committed terrorist acts in the past would be plotting to commit terrorist acts in the future. The second element has to do with attempting to identify terrorists before they become terrorists. This is the predictive aspect of the policy of prevention of terrorism.

The 1978 Foreign Intelligence and Surveillance Act specified the manner in which eavesdropping warrants were to be obtained for the purposes of conducting surveillance against suspected agents of foreign powers and suspected terrorists. In the aftermath of 9/11, members of the Bush administration claimed that FISA hamstrung the ability of law enforcement and intelligence services to conduct surveillance. The reason for the surveillance the government wanted to conduct under FISA was for the purpose of "preventing" terrorism.

After 9/11, preventing terrorism became a top priority of the administration, and five years after 9/11, the Executive Branch published the updated National Strategy for Combating Terrorism. The original national strategy document was published in February 2003. This document outlines the steps that the U.S. Government would take to combat terrorism (National Strategy, 2006).

The White House then published more strategies-the National Strategy to Combat Terrorist Travel, the National Strategy for Maritime Travel, and the National Strategy for Aviation Security. The elements of these strategies that insinuate themselves into a discussion of privacy and surveillance have to do with identity initiatives, and law enforcement and intelligence gathering initiatives.

In the rhetoric surrounding the White House initiative to prevent and disrupt terrorist attacks, the Executive Branch states that the U.S. "law enforcement and intelligence communities must have detailed knowledge of our Homeland adversaries, including their identities, sources of support, intentions, capabilities and modi operandi." ("Prevent and Disrupt," 2007, para. 11) After discussion of collaboration without specifying collaboration between which entities, further explanation leads to a desire to promote the "implementation of Intelligence-Led Policing by State, local, and Tribal law enforcement – after all, they best understand their communities, citizens, and current trend lines." ("Prevent and Disrupt," 2007, para. 12) According to this, the terrorists live in United States communities and not in the Middle East.

Another strategy for counter-terrorist purposes has to do with tracking money as it is moved internationally. The United States has been successful in applying the PATRIOT Act and other laws which apply to banking and transfer of moneys to international banking transactions when the organizations host information in the U.S.

The Society for Worldwide Interbank Financial Transactions (SWIFT) was one such entity affected by U.S. law. In response, the payments processing body announced that it would stop processing European banking transactions in the U.S. in 2009 after criticism from E.U. data protection officials regarding the U.S. surveillance of these transactions. SWIFT officials said they had to turn over data on European citizens' banking transfers because the data was stored in the U.S.

As of 2009, E.U.-U.S. transactions were still hosted in the U.S., and therefore subject to counter-terrorist surveillance, but a new processing center in Switzerland started to process intra-European payment processing ("SWIFT to stop," 2007). In November, 2009, SWIFT data became the subject of a U.S.-E.U. agreement which would still allow U.S. monitoring of financial transaction data, but with some safeguards (Wettstein, 2010).

Another strategy that counter-terrorism experts promote is the idea of predictive data mining, much as the example of the partially assembled needles. This is another example of a strategy that is presented to the public, who are expected to take it on faith. One problem with "predicting" terrorism is that terrorism is a problem with indeterminate boundaries and with which data analysts have only small sample sizes with which to work. Even in commercial applications, data mining produces a very high percentage of false positives. The example given by Jonas and Harper (2006) describes what life would be like if a false positive rate of 1% or even 0.1% were realized (1% and 0.1% are orders of magnitude smaller than real numbers from commercial data mining). In a population of 300,000,000, the FBI would have to investigate 3,000,000 or 300,000 individuals (Jonas & Harper, 2006).

Putting the Local Citizenry under Surveillance

This line of reasoning leads to the recommendation that: "the Federal Government will recommend priorities for State, local and Tribal homeland security activities that focus resources on the most pressing problems, adopt a formal intelligence process with requirements generation and tasking of information collection, and analyze and disseminate the information." ("Prevent and Disrupt," 2007, para. 12) In line with this statement of philosophy, the Federal Government will direct state and local law enforcement in their intelligence collection efforts throughout the Homeland.

There is a critical issue that needs to be addressed in the domestic intelligence community, and question involves, what the criteria used in the development of tasks for local law enforcement is in terms of intelligence gathering. How will information be developed? What information will trigger an investigation? The current set of guiding principles can be discerned from the following:

In order to uncover terrorists and terrorist activity against the backdrop of our highly mobile, dynamic, and diverse society, we must attain domain awareness of the actions, events, and trends that occur throughout our land, maritime, air, space and cyber domains. This is a multi-faceted process. First, partners throughout the entire law enforcement community must continue to enhance their baseline understanding of their operating environments – the people, the geography, and the daily and weekly rhythm of activities and events. By understanding trend lines, we can better identify anomalies and deviations that could indicate terrorist activity. ("Prevent and Disrupt," 2007, para. 11):

The people they are referencing in the document are United States citizens who now are somehow predisposed to become terrorists. The "anomalies and deviations" could be such actions as political protest or groups meeting to discuss how to effect policy change, i.e. legitimate political dissent, as the following example illustrates.

"Undercover Maryland State Police officers repeatedly spied on peace activists and anti-death penalty groups..." (Madigan, 2008, para. 1). 43 pages of documents, much of it redacted, obtained by the ACLU described the infiltration of non-violent groups whose aim was to affect policy change of their government, even thought there was no evidence of criminal or potentially criminal acts. The Maryland State Police conducted surveillance, so far as was discovered, for at least 288 hours over 14 months in 2005 and 2006.

One individual who had drawn government scrutiny was Max Obuszewski. His name is currently in the Washington/Baltimore High Intensity Drug Trafficking Area database.

David Rocah, an ACLU attorney, speaking of the contents of the report, said,

Everything in these logs is a lawful First Amendment Activity. For undercover police officers to spend hundreds of hours entering information about lawful political protest activities into a criminal database is an unconscionable waste of taxpayer dollars and does nothing to make is safer from actual terrorists or drug dealers... Mr. Obuszewski has devoted his entire life to peace. If there is anyone in the world who is further from a terrorist it is hard for me to imagine. (Madigan, 2008, para. 6, 18)

An ACLU policy counsel, Michael German, who is a former FBI agent and who at the FBI was an expert in counter-terrorism, said, "It serves no security purpose to infiltrate peaceful groups. It completely misuses law enforcement resources." (Madigan, 2008, para. 22) Mr. German said that the government has "actively encouraged" local police to gather intelligence and compile information that has no apparent connection to crime.

Mr. Obuszewski seemed puzzled as to the infiltration, explaining that the groups to which he belongs have open meetings and the schedules are publicized. "Why would someone come to those meetings and pretend to be someone else? Why are government agencies targeting pacifists?" he asked (Madigan, 2008, para. 19).

The answer might lie in details of Pentagon surveillance of anti-war groups. NBC News reported that the Department of Defense was collecting information on anti-war protest groups as "potential terrorist threats." (Myers, Pasternak, & Gardella, 2005, p. 2)

The names of the people who participated in meetings were shared with at least seven databases, including the NSA, police departments of Baltimore, Baltimore County, Annapolis and Anne Arundel County, and the state General Services police. The information shared with these agencies and departments were such "terrorist-related" activities as setting up a meeting with then-Representative Benjamin Cardin in 2005 to ask him to support a timetable for withdrawal in Iraq. Other information that is stored on these individuals includes, according to Susan Goering, executive director of the ACLU of Maryland in a letter to Governor Martin O'Malley, "...extensive information about specific individuals and groups, including describing their political outlook, and whether they were articulate, [and] what political activities they are engaged in..." (Madigan, 2008, para. 27).

The information was developed as a result of the state police's Homeland Security and Intelligence Division infiltrating the Baltimore Pledge of Resistance, a peace group, the Committee to Save Vernon Evans, who sits on death row, and the Baltimore Coalition Against the Death Penalty. The fact that the state police has a Homeland Security and Intelligence Division and is infiltrating protest groups is evidence of the seriousness with which law local and state law enforcement are taking their domestic intelligence imperatives.

The state police maintain that they did nothing illegal and they did not curtail protesters' freedoms. Colonel Terrence B. Sheridan, superintendent of the Maryland State Police, went on to say, "Only when information regarding criminal activity is alleged will police continue to investigate leads to ensure the public safety." (Madigan, 2008, para. 9)

The endgame in this type of surveillance is already appearing in the open elsewhere in the industrialized world. The United States government, as just illustrated, was maintaining a database similar to a database in France maintained by its Defense Department equivalent. The database's name is Edvige. The charge of those in France setting up and administering the database is to store data on anyone aged 13 or older who is "likely to breach the public order" (Bremmer, 2008, para. 9) The types of individuals whose information is stored in Edvige includes anyone active in politics or trade unions, as well as those with significant roles in business, the media or entertainment, or social or religious institutions.

Herve Morin, the French Defense Minister, publicly breaking with government policy, questioned the usefulness and role of the database, asking, "Is it useful to gather data such as telephone numbers, sexual orientation and details of taxes and assets and so on without knowing exactly what is the point?" (Bremmer, 2008, para. 6)

This illustrates the manner in which governments all over the world are attempting to equate "breaching the public order" with terrorism. This is the same manner in which the United States Criminal Code is currently constructed, as illustrated earlier, in which civil disobedience, which by definition breaches the public order, is equated with "domestic terrorism." This definition of terrorism may not be the definition with which a civil rights activist in the United States would agree.

The National Strategy for Combating Terrorism describes the endpoint in the war on terrorism in the following terms:

In the War on Terror, there is also a need for all elements of our Nation – from Federal, State and local governments to the private sector to local communities and individual citizens – to help create and share responsibilities in a Culture of Preparedness. This Culture of Preparedness, which applies to all catastrophes and all hazards, natural or man-made, rests on four principles: a shared acknowledgement of the certainty of future catastrophes and that creating a prepared Nation will be a continuing challenge, the importance of initiative and accountability at all levels of society; the role of citizen and community preparedness; and finally, the roles of each level of government and the private sector in creating a prepared Nation. Built upon a foundation of partnerships, common goals and shared responsibility, the creation of a Culture of Preparedness will be among out most profound and enduring transformations in the broader effort to protect and defend the Homeland.(National Strategy, 2006, p. 21).

One of the problems that counter-terrorism operatives face is the problem of individuals who may be terrorists but have not been identified as such. "New recruits, particularly those without criminal records or who are not known to law enforcement, can travel with relative ease from country to country and from city to city with little notice." (Heyman & Carafano, 2008, p. 14) Theoretically, the new powers the government has granted itself will give the counter-terrorists the ability to identify individuals who might not have been identified as terrorists without the new powers.

It is not apparent that there is any assumption that the "Global War on Terror" will ever end. In the literature of those who would defend the taking of powers from the people, there is an assumption that the government will return those powers to the people when the crisis has passed. In the history of the United States in which extraordinary powers have been assumed during times of war and national emergency, some of the rights taken from the people were returned, and some of the additional, extraordinary powers assumed by the government were relinquished at the end of the conflict. Not all of the rights are returned and not all of the powers are relinquished, however.

In the case of the Sedition Act of 1918, the law was repealed, although it was passed again (after World War I was over) and remains in effect to this day. What is important to note, however, is the observation that "Unfortunately, history has shown that it is exponentially harder to wrench power away from the government than it is to give it power in the first place." (Branum, 2001, p. 1)

This particular war may be slightly different, in that there may be no relaxation of the surveillance regime. President Bush declared the war on terror to be "a task that does not end." (G. W. Bush, 2001) Sentiment that the war on terror will never end has been echoed by other members of the Bush administration at various times. President Bush's first national security advisor, in a speech at a U.S. Institute of Peace Conference, compared the war on terror to the war on crime. His sense was that the United States could only win against terrorists "in the sense that we can win the war on crime. We can break its back so that it is a horrible nuisance and not a paralyzing influence on our societies." (Scowcroft, 2002) The Secretary of Defense at the time, Donald Rumsfeld, in response to a question of what the endpoint of the war on terror would look like, said, "I think trying to stamp [terrorism] out in every single locale all across the globe in perpetuity sounds like a pretty big task to me." (Rumsfeld, 2001)

Some surveillance activities are decidedly low-tech, and local police are also emboldened by the knowledge that federal laws permit all manner of information gathering in the context of terrorism investigations. In some cases, local police, even if not specifically tasked with gathering information by a federal intelligence agency, use federal laws as cover for gathering information not normally available to local police under traditional rules of police investigations. Michele Reutty, a librarian, relates the story of the police attempting to access library records to identify a patron by the book the patron was carrying. The police wanted to identify the individual carrying the book as that individual allegedly said something inappropriate to a girl in front of the library.

As the police repeatedly asked for the information on who had checked out which book, Ms. Reutty asked that they follow proper legal procedure and get the proper subpoenas. As the police tried and failed to follow proper legal procedures, pressure was brought to bear on the librarian. She was threatened with the loss of her job. At a board meeting the powers that be were upset that the story had gotten national attention and that the borough clerk and the police department were getting calls supporting Ms. Reutty's position that the police get the proper subpoena before she would turn the information over to the police. In this particular instance, the incident catapulted her into a new job and provided the impetus for libraries throughout New Jersey to develop a policy for librarians to follow when the police arrive with requests for patron records (Reutty, 2007).

Knowledge of terrorists' and "potential terrorists'" movements is of use to counter-terrorists and law enforcement, and this type of surveillance is best accomplished with a regime in which individuals can be identified and tracked with some degree of accuracy. The 9/11 Commission recommended that the government in the future stipulate that driver's licenses should become more reliable as indicators of individuals' identities (9/11_Commission, 2004).

A good link between the identity the individual has on file with the government and the items which are chipped, i.e., have RFID embedded, provides a useful way to track those individuals. Tracking is easier if one of the chipped items is a government issued ID card. The government contends that the ID along with the other powers it has seized will provide success in the GWOT.

An illustration of successes in the Global War on Terror attributed to the new powers the government granted itself comes from a government report. This 2004 report prepared by the U.S. Department of Justice (*Report From the Field*, 2004) details the effects the use of the powers granted in the PATRIOT Act had in the disruption and prevention of terrorist attacks, specifically, the case of the "Lackawanna Six."

The Lackawanna Six had traveled to an al-Qaeda camp outside Kandahar in Afghanistan, a Taliban stronghold. According to the Justice Department report, the government was tipped off to the presence of home-grown terrorists by an anonymous letter. The report also made much of the intelligence "wall" that kept law enforcement personnel investigating agents of foreign powers and those investigating common criminals from communicating when the investigation began in the summer of 2001, saying, "...there were times when the intelligence officers and the law enforcement agents concluded that they could not be in the same room during briefings to discuss their respective investigations with each other." (*Report From the Field*, 2004, p. 3)

The situation was not new for law enforcement and intelligence services. The PATRIOT Act and other laws which followed were desired by the law enforcement and intelligence communities for years prior to the attacks of 9/11.

In May 1995, a report was written for the Attorney General and the Director of Central Intelligence in response to the Banca Nazionale del Lavoro (BNL) and Bank of Credit and Commerce International (BCCI) prosecutions in the early 1990's. The report stated that, "Greater cooperation between law enforcement and intelligence, and better-focused participation by LEA's in proposing intelligence requirements, will lead to better use of existing resources." (Report to the Attorney General, 1995, p. 15)

The origin of these problems is said to be traced back to the "Wall" memo that was written by the Attorney General at the time, Janet Reno, on July 19, 1995.One of the provisions in the memo concerned contact between a Foreign Intelligence (FI) or Foreign Counter-Intelligence (FCI) Investigation and the Justice Department in the circumstance in which no Foreign Intelligence Surveillance Act (FISA) surveillance or searches were being conducted. The memo stated that, "The FBI shall not contact a U.S. Attorney's Office concerning such an investigation…" (Reno, 1995, p. Sec. B.2)

With the passage of the PATRIOT Act, the two teams of investigators were able to communicate and the case ended with five of the six pleading guilty to providing material support to al-Qaeda and the sixth pleading guilty to "conducting transactions unlawfully" with al-Qaeda. The prison sentences meted out were between seven and ten years for these offenses. (*Report From the Field*, 2004)

Other successes due to the removal of the "Wall" include the cases of the "Portland Seven." In this case, Jeffrey Battle, one of the conspirators, had discussed the terrorist plot he was working on with an undercover informant.

Others in the cell had traveled to Pakistan to take up arms with al-Qaeda against the United States and coalition forces. When they were unsuccessful in their quest, they returned to the United States. The FBI was empowered, through sections 218 and 504 of the Patriot Act, to put these individuals under surveillance while a case was being built, and then capture them before they could commit any terrorism. Six were sent to prison, receiving sentences of three to 18 years each, and the last, Jaber Elbaneh, was killed by Pakistani troops in Pakistan, or at least according to the 2004 report. The latest news has Jaber Elbaneh at large in Yemen, and on the FBI list of "most wanted terrorists." (Temple-Rastin, 2007a)

Other successes detailed by the government included the successful arrests and/or prosecutions of Sami Al-Arian and co-conspirators in a case of Palestinian Islamic Jihad (PIJ), defendants in the "Virginia Jihad" case, in which the terrorists were associated with an Islamic extremist group known as Lashkar-e-Taiba (LET) and the cases of Mohammed Ali Hasan Al-Moayed and Mohshen Yahya Zayed, both Yemeni citizens, for their involvement with al Qaeda and HAMAS (*Report From the Field*, 2004).

Additional successfully prosecuted cases involved racketeers using charities as front groups for support for Chechen rebels; an al Qaeda related drugs-for-weapons plot, and a spying case involving an agent of the former Iraqi government. In all of these cases, the PATRIOT Act was cited as making the difference between success and failure in investigating and prosecuting the cases (*Report From the Field*, 2004).

Finally, cases in which the PATRIOT Act has figured prominently involve money transfer and laundering, including cases involving the Columbian rebel group FARC, an arms dealer and operators of unlicensed money transmitting businesses. Additional successes have been achieved in seizing the money and property of terrorists and those with whom they did business. The gist of the report, however had more to do with the success of tearing down the intelligence/law enforcement "Wall," and the imposition of stiffer penalties for criminal acts than with any successes of data-mining or surveillance initiatives purchasing the government more in the way of convictions (*Report From the Field*, 2004).

The parallels with anti-terrorism activities in the most surveilled Western democracy, Great Britain, are substantial. The British have the type of camera surveillance build out that law enforcement in the

United States would like to have (Hope, 2008; Temple-Rastin, 2007b). The Fusion Center concept is based on and builds on the Intelligence-Led Policing (ILP) model. Due to the international nature of information sharing among intelligence and law enforcement communities of cooperating countries, initiatives and experiences from Great Britain and the United States cross the Atlantic and therefore create elements of common experience.

The subway bombings in Britain on July 17, 2005 were examples of the importance to the government of surveillance of their citizens, even though the surveillance did nothing to prevent the attack.

Three bombs exploded in the London subway system at 0720 BST, and one on a bus at 0947 BST, killing 51 innocent people plus the four bombers ("Images," 2005). The Intelligence and Security Committee report released in March, 2006 put the death toll at 52 as one additional injured person died from wounds.

The Prime Minister at the time, Tony Blair, made a statement on July 11th of that year to say that he knew of "no intelligence specific enough to have allowed then to prevent last Thursday's attacks." (*Report into the London Terrorist Attacks*, 2006) With this dismissive wave of his hand, the Prime Minister removed emphasis on the question of how the government can prevent terror attacks and why the attacks were not prevented.

The report quotes from a speech by Dame Eliza Manningham-Buller to the Dutch security forces at The Hague, reported in Lord Butler's Review of Intelligence on Weapons of Mass Destruction (2003-2004), as follows:

> The Agencies cannot know everything about everyone, nor can they intercept and read every communication (which in any event would be a gross violation of human rights.) There will always be gaps in the Agencies' knowledge.

The implication is that if the intelligence agencies could intercept and analyze all of everyone's communications, then terrorism could be prevented. The report goes on to discuss the enormous volume of information generated in investigating terrorism, how the U.K. security forces have foiled other plots (and can't say which ones) but didn't foil this one, and the question of the manner in which intelligence is to be prioritized.

One of the bombers was known to have traveled to Pakistan in 2003 and at the time the report was issued, there was no clear connection to international terrorists in terms of external direction and planning (*Report into the London Terrorist Attacks*, 2006, p. 12). It was later established that the bombing was masterminded by Abu Ubaida al-Masri (an alias) of Pakistan and top al-Qaeda leader ("Top Al Qacda Leader," 2008).

The U.K. Security Service had previously had contact with two of the bombers, Siddeque Khan and Shazad Tanweer, the bombers being on the periphery of other investigations (*Rcport into the London Terrorist Attacks*, 2006, p. 14) The Security Service was absolved of responsibility for supposing to have known to prevent the attacks. The fact that these bombers had been identified from surveillance or terrorist activities and they were not prevented from committing terrorism does not seem to matter. The terrorists were left alone. London is one of the most closely monitored cities in the world. Investigators worked for four days going over the camera data from the 3,000 cameras in the London subway system to try to find evidence of the suicide bombers' movements (Milcent & Cai, 2006). After the fact, it was not claimed that surveillance could have prevented the attack. Yet the government calls for more surveillance under a theory that more surveillance could prevent future attacks.

The British government attempted to legalize building a database that will contain all of everyone's communications. The reason given involved having the ability to stop terrorism before it happens (Prince, 2008). Communication data in the United States already exists, in ISP record phone records. With the new FBI guidelines, these are de facto government databases. The FBI can access these records with National Security Letters. There is no judicial oversight and the FBI needs no probable cause to open an investigation on anyone. Therefore, the data is freely available to the FBI for any purpose at any time with or without a real reason (Johnson, 2008; Jordan, 2007).

The question becomes, how much surveillance is enough? Who should be put under surveillance? The answer advanced by the government of the United States is to monitor everyone. Monitoring and tracking everyone is also the answer for the government of Britain. The British are building a huge DNA database. DNA is the most information-rich and personal biometric. The government of Britain had populated the database with data from everyone over the age of 10 who has is arrested. Those whose DNA is catalogued and stored include those who are not charged. The database also includes the DNA of those who are charged but found innocent. There are now 4.5 million genetic samples in the British DNA database (Townsend & Asthana, 2008). The FBI is also building a massive biometric database (Nakashima, 2007).

There is a call in the United States to install a video surveillance system similar in size and scope to that in Great Britain. On the Fourth of July, 2007, National Public Radio broadcast a story about American police chiefs who want the type of surveillance power that the British have. There are enough cameras in Britain, 4,285,000 in 2008 (Hope, 2008) that Scotland Yard can track the movement of every single car in the country. (Hope, 2008) Current capabilities allow that the system can store the data for two years.

Miami Police Chief John Timoney used to believe that the surveillance powers a network of cameras that vast represented was too intrusive and that, "...I was opposed to it" (Temple-Rastin, 2007b, para. 6 & 12). Not anymore. Now he and William Bratton, police chief in Los Angeles, feel these are the tools needed by law enforcement to fight terrorism. There was no mention of the predictive capability that these cameras might give police, but Bratton was impressed with the idea that not just individuals but groups could be identified after the fact as they went places to commit terrorism (Temple-Rastin, 2007b, para 12).

Chief Timoney contended that civil libertarians are exaggerating the problems with this type of surveillance. Barry Steinhardt of the ACLU pointed out that the amount of money spent on taking pictures of streets and highways and using those pictures to track people and vehicles would be better spent on investigating and apprehending terrorists. Mr. Steinhardt is also concerned about potential abuses such as tracking innocent people and the police using the camera's abilities for other than its intended purpose, such as "looking for attractive women." . But Chief Timoney feels that "most of these concerns have been dealt with." (Temple-Rastin, 2007b, para 16)

While it may be true that police have misused the resources at their command for personal purposes in the past, the amount of information aggregated in the databases created after 9/11 is immense. In the past, where the police might have had lists of drivers license numbers and home addresses, the current generation of information aggregation and correlation systems, such as Seisint's Matrix, store and can connect much more in the way of social networking information (O'Harrow, 2005) thereby putting additional individuals at risk for police abuse.

In the case of Collier County, Florida, it was a lucky break that allowed a problem like that to be "dealt with." Terri Lucas in the Fingerprinting Department at the Collier County Sheriff's Office was fired for unauthorized access to the DAVID system, the database for driver and vehicle information when she looked up her ex-boyfriend's current girlfriend. The break in the case came when the current girlfriend notified police. Lucas said she looked up "a ton of people...for fun...We used it like a yearbook." The department plans to start running audits against "unusual activity" so that these types of problems can be dealt with (Spinetto, 2008).

An interesting aside in the matter of the London bombing case was the attempt to convict three men for helping to scout locations and training with the bombers, as well as being connected to the apartments in which the home-made explosives were mixed. The government used cell phone tracking data and surveillance footage for travel around London on December 16 and 17, 2004, to show that the accomplices went to the London Eye and Natural History Museum. Prosecutors said the itinerary "bore a striking similarity" to the bombers' travels on the day they blew up the train cars and the bus (Stobart & Rotella, 2008, para. 9). The buried lead is that the cell phone tracking data existed for the suspects. Therefore, everyone's tracking data is saved all the time, and is possibly held indefinitely. It's all up to the cell phone company.

An example of an unsuccessful prosecution because of government lies in the United States was the case of one of the "sleeper cell" prosecutions. This story made the news when Attorney General John Ashcroft announced the arrests of four Muslim men in Detroit. Unfortunately for the sleeper cell narrative, the charges were dropped quietly when Richard Coventino, prosecutor of the case, was indicted for attempting to enter false evidence into the record, and concealing other evidence (Wolf, 2007, p. 10).

Infiltration

One of the tactics the FBI has been instructed to (re-)adopt is that of infiltration. FBI informants infiltrating, spying on, and in some cases agitating and inciting otherwise peaceful, lawful, protest organizations was one of the strategies that was decried in the Church Committee hearings and subsequently outlawed. A fact of relevance in the wake of the Church Committee Hearings and the fate of the Intelligence Oversight Board that was set up in response to the findings of lawlessness in the law enforcement and intelligence community is that in the recent past, the powers of that board have been severely limited by President Bush. (Savage, 2008)

President Gerald Ford created the Intelligence Oversight Board as a response to the 1975-1976 investigation by Congress into domestic spying, assassination attempts and other intelligence agency abuses. President Ford's executive order creating the board took effect March 1, 1976. Almost 32 years to the day of its creation, President Bush limited its powers with an order issued February 29 (G. Bush, 2008), in a move which the timing of was termed "purely coincidental" by the White House. (Savage, 2008, para. 8)

One major change to the board's operation was such that in the past, the board was to inform the President and the Attorney General when an intelligence activity was thought to have been "unlawful or contrary to executive order." (Savage, 2008, para. 9) Now, the board is not to refer anything to the Justice Department independently, and only to inform the president if other officials were not "adequately" addressing the problem. Also, the board no longer has oversight of each agency's general counsel and inspector general, and instead of each inspector general being required to file a report with the board each quarter, each agency director has the discretion to report law-breaking to the board at those directors' discretion, with no schedule for notification (Savage, 2008).

Weakening the Intelligence Oversight Board was merely the latest in a series of actions throughout Bush's terms that have limited and weakened restrictions on intelligence agency activities. Another change allows the NSA to gather information about Americans by using other agencies to collect the information. Assassinations, which were once prohibited, are sanctioned. Wiretap laws and policies have been significantly weakened. Congress had a law on the books requiring that the full House and Senate intelligence committees be briefed about spying activities, but the administration has determined that only the committee leadership needs to be briefed. And executive orders were once thought to be in force until rescinded, yet the Bush administration has secretly authorized members of the intelligence community to ignore certain executive orders, without actually rescinding the orders. (Savage, 2008)

One of the operations to which the creation of the Intelligence Oversight Board was a reaction was the COunter INTELligence PROgram (COINTELPRO.) COINTELPRO was an FBI operation which used agents and informers to infiltrate and discredit civil rights groups, anti-war groups and other groups whose interests were inimical to the established power structure. For example, on April 22, 1970, the FBI was there when 20 million Americans participated in Earth Day. Agents in 40 cities were ordered to spy on Earth Day gatherings and report on individuals and groups which planned and participated in the Earth Day events. The goal of the FBI was to link the individuals and groups in attendance to organizations which were targeted for "surveillance, infiltration and disruption." (D. Cole & Dempsey, 2002, p. 7)

That Earth Day, the FBI in Denver was diligent about recording Senator Gaylord Nelson's utterances, and had written down each of the slogans on the signs that protesters carried. In general, however, the FBI ended up investigating civil rights activists, Vietnam War protesters, women's liberation advocates and other protest groups. Some of the more innovative FBI tactics included spreading misinformation about groups, inciting illegal activity and generally trying to discredit the groups and in general bring discouragement to the members of those groups (D. Cole & Dempsey, 2002).

Surveillance and Interdiction on the Internet

In the U.S. strategy for combating terrorism, one of the venues in which the war on terror is to be fought is the Internet. The United States' policy is clearly stated, in that, "We will seek ultimately to deny the Internet to the terrorists as an effective safehaven (sic) for their propaganda, proselytizing, recruitment, fundraising, training and operational planning." (National Strategy, 2006, p. 17) An example of success in that arena is illustrated by the fact that someone, the government would not say who, took down various al-Qaeda sites prior to the anniversary of 9/11.

Al Qaeda had been using five main online forums to deliver their messages. All five of these were taken off-line on September 10th, 2008. The next day only one was back up and others were scrambling. The anniversary message did not appear until September 19th, and by then it was not as effective for the terrorist group. This was a serious blow to al-Qaeda's propaganda effort, as al-Qaedahad been hyping the appearance of a video in the weeks prior to the seventh anniversary of the World Trade Center attacks.

U.S. intelligence sources would not say if the U.S. government was behind the attacks, although some speculated that it might have been an independent effort by Web "vigilantes." Erich Marquardt, of the Combating Terrorism Center at the U.S. Military Academy at West Point, said, "The downside of knocking jihadist Web sites offline is that you lose the ability to monitor jihadist activities." (Knickmeyer, 2008) Clearly then, even the most "obvious" anti-terror strategies may have a downside.

In this case, monitoring the Web site for information about that which the jihadists are thinking is different than tracking American citizens' as they go about their daily routines, and thus has value and is a wise use of resources. And, unlike the average American who might join a protest organization or social justice group, some terrorists have more in common with common Internet criminals than social activists.

One example of cybercrime by terrorists to raise money is the theft of data by a group of three men. Tariq al-Daour, 21, Waseem Mughal, 24, and Younes Tsouli, 23 pleaded guilty in Britain in the summer of 2007 to charges related to inciting terrorism, specifically to using the

Internet to incite murder. What they were really guilty of, however, was a series of cybercrimes involving stolen credit cards numbers taken from victims in phishing attacks.

Phishing is the practice of sending emails which contain a link to a site that looks to be a legitimate site, but in fact steals the credentials that the victim might input at a legitimate site. at the bogus site. For instance, someone might get an email with a link to a site purporting to need information to "verify" their account status, or avoid "cancellation" of a service ("Phishing Explained," n.d.). This type of attack, and in general, attacks that are not strictly technical in nature, but instead require a person to be tricked, are called "social engineering" attacks (Granger, 2001)

In the case of the three terrorists who pled guilty in Britain, one of the individuals who fell prey to the "social engineering" attack was Linda Spence of New Jersey. She entered information into a counterfeit eBay site, and subsequently her credit card was used for $2,000 in fraudulent charges to a business in Portugal. The bad guys in this particular case used 72 or more stolen credit card accounts and registered more than 180 World Wide Web domain names at 95 hosting companies in the United States and Europe. These sites were then used to spread jihadist propaganda and terrorism information (Krebs, 2007).

Another issue that has Western security experts concerned involves applications that would normally be considered tools strictly for hackers and criminals, which are available on the Internet. When these tools are modified and crafted to suit the ambitions of terrorists, however, there is an added dimension of danger.

The "electronic jihad" site, Al-jinan.org, was a terrorist site taken off line in the summer of 2007. It illustrates the problems of security on the Internet in an age of terror, as well as the ability of terrorist sites to avoid detection, even in plain sight.

Al-jinan.org has an application for download named "Electronic Jihad." The purpose of the computer program is to attack Western sites by using what is known as a denial-of-service attack (DoS). DoS attacks are most well-known currently in the form of distributed denial of service attacks, (DDoS), which are generally attributed to botnets. Botnets have been in the news as botnets consist of regular individuals' and organizations' computers which have become infected with malevolent software (called malware), which allows the infected computers to be controlled by criminals. Under the criminal control they can launch DDoS attacks (Glenn, 2003).

DoS (and DDoS) attacks attempt to take a target Web site off line by overwhelming the bandwidth or server resources with legitimate looking requests, such as for Web pages. When the volume of these requests is too great, the Web site is unreachable for legitimate users (Glenn, 2003).

The software at al-Jinan.org was not particularly effective for the purposes for which it was written. Security experts, see a day when attempts by terrorists to craft applications for similar purposes would not be so feeble.. Jordan Wiens, senior security engineer for the University of Florida, put it best when he expressed concern as to what might happen if "if they ever get their act together." (Greenemeier, 2007, para 8)

.

CHAPTER 4:

Technology of the Real ID Act

What is the Real ID Act?

The Real ID Act was passed as part of Public Law 109-13, with the full title "Making Emergency Supplemental Appropriations for Defense, the Global War on Terror, and Tsunami Relief, for the fiscal year ending September 30, 2005, and for other purposes." The Act has the short title "Emergency Supplemental Appropriations Act for Defense, the Global War on Terror, and Tsunami Relief, 2005." ("Real ID Act," 2005)

The Real ID Act is Division B of the Act. Title I concerns barring terrorists entry to the United States. Title II is "Improved Security for Drivers' Licenses and Personal Identification Cards." ("Real ID Act," 2005) The Act was signed into law by President George W. Bush on May 11, 2005 (G. Bush, 2005). There was no mention in the President's signing statement of the Real ID provisions of the bill, which meant that the White House would enforce all of the provisions of that part of the Act. The Real ID Act started out as H.R. 418, entitled, "To establish and rapidly implement regulations for State drivers' license and identification document security standards, to prevent terrorists from abusing the asylum laws of the United States, to unify terrorism-related grounds for inadmissibility and removal, and to ensure expeditious construction of the San Diego border fence." The bill was then appended as Division B to H.R. 1268, which became Public Law 109-13 when it was passed ("H.R. 418 - THOMAS (Library of Congress)," 2005).

The original Real ID Act, as H.R. 418, was sponsored by Representative F. James Sensenbrenner and introduced on January 26, 2005. At that time, he was Chairman of the House Committee on the Judiciary ("Congressman Sensenbrenner," n.d.).

There are several aspects of the Real ID Act which deserve consideration. The wording of the Act is vague on the manner in which the goal of the Act is to be achieved. The goal of the Act is that licenses are to be made more secure, and the rule-making fell under the purview of DHS. There was contention regarding the rules and whether RFID was to be used. The current rules do not specify RFID as the vehicle for the machine-readable format. However, critics, among them State Representative Jim Guest of Missouri, contend that the bar code format currently specified could be changed by DHS by fiat to RFID with no meaningful input nor oversight .

What is a Real ID?

A Real ID is a driver's license that conforms to the rules issued by the Department of Homeland Security (DHS) in 6 CFR Part 37, the Federal Register of January 29, 2008, pp. 5271-5340, entitled, "Minimum Standards for Driver's Licenses and Identification Cards Acceptable by Federal Agencies for Official Purposes; Final Rule." All of the following descriptions of what the Real ID consists and procedures for issuing the ID, including the format and description of the actual document are contained in the Final Rule.

The rules are constructed to dictate to the states that on a series of dates, the Federal government will no longer accept state-issued IDs that don't conform to the Real ID rules. For instance, states must have applied for a waiver (extension) on conforming to the federally mandated standard by March 31, 2008, which all of the states did. As of December 31, 2009, if a state had not complied with the terms of the Material Compliance Checklist and not applied for another extension by October 11, 2009, the federal government would not accept those states' citizen's IDs for federal purposes. And on May 11, 2011, the federal government would not accept IDs from states determined to not be in compliance with Real ID. However, the Federal Register of December 28, 2009 shows that 37.51, paragraph (b), which had mandated the December 31, 2009 deadline, was stayed from January 1, 2010 until further notice ("Rules and Regulations / Vol.74, No. 247 / 68478," 2009).

On December 1, 2014, those born after 1964 must have a Real ID, and December 1, 2017, the final group, everyone, is to have been checked and verified. Anyone without a Real ID will not be allowed to board an airplane, go into a nuclear power plant, enter a federal building, or "such other purposes as established by the Secretary of Homeland Security" (*Minimum Standards*, 2008, p. 5273) It is anyone's guess as to what the Secretary of the Department of Homeland Security might dictate. And dictate is the correct characterization according to Jim Guest. As State Representative Jim Guest of Missouri notes, there is neither judicial nor legislative oversight for implementation of this Act (Ferguson, 2007, para. 9).

Most people will not be inconvenienced much by not being allowed into a nuclear power plant. However, the rules make for the interesting possible situation of an American citizen being denied the ability to petition the Federal Government for redress of grievances if they don't have their Real ID. Considering the fact that 20 percent of all ID instruments are lost each year (Schneier, 2007b) it would be inconvenient to actually have gotten it then have it stolen the night before the big court case.

The states shoulder the responsibility for ensuring the validity of source documents which verify the identity of the individual. DHS has mandated rules for document retention which the states must implement. Source documents which are on paper, if stored by the state, are to be kept for seven years. Microfiche and digital images of source documents are to be retained for ten years and all the documents or their images must be retrievable by DMV if properly requested by law enforcement (*Minimum Standards*, 2008, p. 5337) Most states would, for economy's sake, scan the documents and store them in computer storage. This computer storage of birth certificates and other documents creates a target-rich environment for hackers.

The ID card itself must have a 2D bar code as the machine readable zone (MRZ). The MRZ will contain a copy of the information printed on the driver's license. The card shall include the holder's full name and address, date of birth and gender, the card's number, and the person's signature. A digital photograph is mandated, either color or black and white. The 2D bar code format specified is the PDF417 format in use by many law enforcement agencies today, and without encryption. This allows for easy access to the information by law enforcement and anyone with a bar code reader. 2D bar code readers are quite common. Airport boarding passes contain 2D bar codes ("Bar coded," n.d.) so there is a reader at every gate. A 2-D bar code card reader can be had for $150-$300 as of October, 2010, so there is little financial impediment to obtaining the capability to read bar coded IDs ("CS101," n.d.).

Is Real ID an Unfunded Mandate?

Some of the tension between the states and the federal government has to do with the "voluntary" nature of the provisions of the Act and whether it is indeed something with which the states are to voluntary comply, or if compliance can be considered to be mandatory. If it is not voluntary, as some critics contend, due to the draconian penalties for non-conformance by the states, then it becomes an unfunded mandate. Some states contend that the expense of administration to comply with the Act is onerous and that the Act amounts to an unfunded mandate. Unite States Senator Kahikina Akaka (D-Hawaii) said, "The Act places a significant unfunded mandate on states..." (Understanding the Realities of REAL ID: A Review of Efforts to Secure Drivers Licenses and Identification Cards, 2007) James Harper of the Cato Institute, a libertarian think tank in Washington, D.C., in his testimony before the Senate Judiciary Committee, described the Real ID Act as an unfunded mandate (*Real ID Act Hearings*, 2007).

During the late 1970s and early 1980s, mandates were a popular topic of study. At that time, state officials were vocal in their dissatisfaction with federal mandates that were not funded with commensurate federal aid or grants to the states (MacManus, 1991).

Intergovernmental tension is fueled by the imposition of imperatives on lower levels of government by levels of government above, without the necessary funding to achieve the mandated condition (Leckrone, 1997). The imposition of unfunded mandates is not necessarily uniquely federal to state in nature. The intergovernmental tensions were felt in the state to county hierarchy to such a degree that by 1990, with the addition of Florida and Wisconsin, ten states had constitutionally mandated reimbursement provisions and eight states had statutory requirements to reimburse local governments for state mandates (MacManus, 1991). By 1998, totals had grown to 12 states with constitutional and 13 with statutory provisions regarding mandates (Nobles, 2000).

In 1995, the Unfunded Mandate Reform Act (UMRA) was signed into law, which had as its stated purpose, "...to strengthen the partnership between federal, state, local and tribal governments by ensuring that the impact of legislative and regulatory proposals on those governments are given full consideration in Congress and the Executive Branch before they are acted on." (Leckrone, 1997, p. par 4)

In hearings conducted in May of 2007 by the Senate Committee on the Judiciary, Senator Patrick Leahy (D-Vermont) and Senator Arlen Spectre (R-Pennsylvania) both quoted the DHS estimate of costs to the states for compliance as $23 billion (*Real ID Act Hearings*, 2007, pp. 2-3). In September of 2007 that estimate had been revised down to $11 billion over five years (Lipowicz, 2007).

At a press conference announcing the final rules for Real ID, Michael Chertoff continued to put pressure on states to comply. Secretary Chertoff threatened that if individuals are carrying ID from states which did not comply nor intend to comply with the Real ID Act, those individuals would not be allowed to fly on commercial airlines, nor to access federal buildings (Chertoff, 2008b).

A selling point for Real ID as the Secretary tells the story is that the adoption of Real ID will help ameliorate the illegal immigration problem. The contention being that illegal aliens use Social Security Numbers of citizens, thus presenting a fraud and identity theft problem (Chertoff, 2006b) and that the use of Real ID will solve that problem. Secretary Chertoff also made the case for expanding the scope of use for Real ID for employment purposes, by integrating the information that employers checked against Basic Pilot/E-Verify with the Real ID distributed database. Basic Pilot, now rebranded as E-Verify, is a program of cooperation between the Social Security Administration and the Immigration and Custom Enforcement department of DHS which allows employers to check Social Security Numbers to see if they match the names that applicants provide ("DHS Basic Pilot," 2008) Secretary Chertoff asserts that Basic Pilot does not indicate if that Social Security Number is possibly being used in multiple employment situations, but that if the database used for identification were used in conjunction with the Real ID database, having been referred for action through DHS, this would protect people from identity theft (Chertoff, 2006b, para.16-19). This explanation begs the question as to how the system would provide protection against identity theft if multiple employment situations are not flagged.

Other mandates to the states for compliance with the Real ID Act include deadlines for compliance, and privacy and data security considerations. States' rights adherents and civil libertarians observe that national identity cards are anathema to the citizens' sense of the role of the federal government. Even as DHS has pushed the deadlines back, the Secretary of the Department of Homeland Security foretold of severe punishment for the residents of the states that would not comply with the Act. The same punishment had been envisioned to be meted out to states that missed even the deadlines for requesting extensions for compliance dates.

In the final rules as DHS released them, states had until May 11, 2008 to either comply with the Real ID Act or request a waiver for extension of the deadline. After that date, individuals from states that were not in compliance nor had applied for a waiver of compliance would be subject to "secondary" treatment at airports and upon entering federal facilities. This would entail pat-down searches (Singel, 2008a) and the necessity of DHS to perform some type of verification of the identity of those individuals. This type of situation would also cause delays, which Secretary Chertoff hypothesized would translate into dissatisfaction of the citizens with their non-compliant state governments, and thus promote compliance (Chertoff, 2008).

Privacy advocates claim that the Real ID Act's inclusion in the Tsunami Relief and Defense Appropriations Bill was done stealthily and the time frame was such that it was only a matter of days before the vote that those civil libertarians who would oppose the Act even knew it was included, limiting their ability to respond and attempt to remove the Real ID portion from the larger bill. Twelve Senators went so far as to write a letter to then-Senate Majority Leader Bill Frist urging that the Real ID portion of the Act not be included in the larger appropriation bill, but to no avail ("Twelve Senators," 2005).

In addition to the features of the Real ID cards described earlier, there is another component to compliance with the Act. Concurrent with the issuance of the cards with the 2D bar codes, the individual's identity information would be stored in a database in each state. This data would be stored in a format such that the databases for each state could communicate for lookup purposes with each other state, and such that all states would have database formats that would be interoperable between all other states ("Real ID Draft Regulations," 2007).

Timing and Implementation Complications

Real ID Advocates, including Michael Chertoff, and in the testimony to the Senate Judiciary Committee, Janice Kephart of 9/11 Security Solutions, LLC, suggest that the driver's license provisions in the Real ID Act are superior to the driver's license provisions in the Intelligence Reform and Terrorism Prevention Act of 2004. The Senators at the hearing, expressed concern regarding the fact that the Real ID Act was pushed through in an authorization bill without hearings. The question had to do with what made Real ID superior in the security requirements for driver's licenses to those in Public Law 108-458, the Intelligence Reform and Terrorism Prevention Act of 2004, which had gone through the hearing process and was considered to be well-considered in those provisions. It was thought that the provisions in Public Law 108-458 were in line with the 9/11 Commission recommendations ("Intelligence Reform and Terrorism Prevention Act of 2004," 2004).

A close reading of Section 7212 of Public Law 108-458 of 2004 reveals that the most significant difference regards the mandate for a national distributed, searchable database. The Intelligence Reform Act does not require such a database, whereas the Real ID Act requires that database to be implemented ("Real ID Act of 2005," 2005, p. 50). The database requirement is known in the Act as the "Driver License Agreement" (DLA). Another difference is the Real ID Act's requirement to cross-check the individual's identity against the database of Social Security numbers ("Real ID Act of 2005," 2005). The DLA does not extend only to the states and federal government, but also to "…those provinces and territories in Canada and those states in Mexico that join the DLA and comply with its provisions. While it's not specifically stated, other countries could join the DLA, which would mandate reciprocity of information on potentially a global scale." (Ferguson, 2007)

Another significant difference between the driver's license provisions in the Real ID Act and those in the Intelligence Reform and

Terrorism Prevention Act of 2004 exists. This is that the rule-making falls solely under the purview of the Department of Homeland Security. This scuttles the provisions of the 2004 Act which had the states and the federal government working together to arrive at standards for driver's license security.

There was confusion when the law was passed as to what mechanism would be used to as the machine readable format for the Real ID card. Many in the industry at the time thought that RFID would be the front-running technology (Ferguson, 2007), as passports were being redesigned and issued with RFID chips starting on August 14, 2006 (Ezovski & Watkins, 2007).

The entire story of the Real ID Act is unusual for many reasons. One would expect that there would be consensus in the passage of a law which would help keep the American public safer. It appears, however the Real ID Act is something that is being forced on the people of the United States, as demonstrated in the threatening stance taken by representatives of DHS.

Secretary Chertoff did nothing to dispel the notion that DHS was using heavy-handed tactics in dictating to the states the manner and timing with which the Real ID Act was to be implemented. In an editorial published soon after the final rules were released, dismissing criticism of the manner in which the rules were to be implemented, he wrote, "A good example is the spurious claim that we're ushering in a national identity card. What we are actually doing is setting standards that will *let the states keep issuing their own ID cards.*" (emphasis added) (Chertoff, 2008a) The implication is that even though this is not a national ID card, that if the states do not follow the mandate, they would not be able to continue to issue their own ID cards.

Throughout the process of attempting to get the Real ID initiative off the ground, there has been confusion regarding the deadlines and with what parts of the law states were to comply and when.

On September 10, 2007, Secretary Chertoff told the Senate Committee on Homeland Security and Governmental Affairs that the states were originally given a deadline of October 1, 2007 to comply even as the final rules had not been issued yet at that time. That date was moved back to the end of 2009 for states requesting a waiver (Lipowicz, 2007). But adding to the confusion was the fact that in the meantime, May of 2008 was set as a deadline for having all states either come into compliance with Real ID, or apply for a waiver. In November 2007, Secretary Chertoff revealed a new timetable. This convoluted timetable would have given the states' until 2013 to bring 245 million U.S. drivers' licenses into compliance with the Real ID Act. Then the target date would become 2018 for drivers older than 40, or 50 (DHS hadn't made up the states' mind yet) to be issued Real ID compliant licenses (Hsu, 2007b).

At that time, Timothy Sparapani, senior legislative counsel for the American Civil Liberties Union noted that DHS was continually weakening the program to attempt to gain compliance. Sparapani said, "DHS is doing back flips in order to get states to say they are complying with Real ID." (Hsu, 2007b)

Secretary Chertoff and DHS had set a compliance date for the states of May, 2008, even before the Notice of Proposed Rulemaking (NPRM) had been issued. The NPRM appeared in the Federal Register on March 9, 2007 ("Real ID Draft Regulations," 2007). Yet in February of 2007, Michael Chertoff testified to the Senate Homeland Security and Governmental Affairs Committee and said he was "pretty adamant" about a May, 2008 deadline. Senator Susan Collins (R-Maine), was considering sponsoring an amendment giving the states more time. She observed, "It has been two years since the Real ID Act passed, and yet we don't have detailed regulations or guidance from the department setting forth the standards that the states are going to have to follow." (Hudson, 2007)

Secretary Chertoff made the point that privacy and security were paramount and said, "I do want to make it clear that one of the reasons it's taking awhile is we have actually done quite a bit of consultation even in the preliminary stage with state officials and privacy advocates and other folks." (Hudson, 2007, par 10) Secretary Chertoff never enumerates who the privacy advocates and "other folks" might be. A reasonable person might presume that because the program is a security program and security of the data and the computers holding the data is important, the "other folks" might be computer and information security professionals.

The Race/Ethnicity Field

Secretary Chertoff left the door open for the inclusion of biometric identifiers – beyond the digital photo requirement. Each driver's license will have at a minimum a digital photograph as the biometric identifier. As the Secretary indicated at the press conference upon release of the final rules for compliance with the Act, DHS was not opposed to other biometric identifiers being included on the ID (or in the database), "We have nothing against a fingerprint. Some states have fingerprints, some states don't." (Chertoff, 2008b)

The Act does not specify that a race field be included, nor filled. In addition to the digital photograph, the Act mandates the individual's full legal name, date of birth, gender, driver's license number, address and signature ("Real ID Act of 2005," 2005). The Act mandates that the machine-readable portion contain common data elements. This is of special concern for civil libertarians as there is a race field is in the specification for the machine-readable portion of the Real ID that DHS has picked for implementation. At the time Jim Harper spoke to the Senate Committee on Homeland Security and Governmental Affairs, subcommittee on Oversight of Government Management, the Federal Workforce, and the District of Columbia on March 26, 2007, the Notice of Proposed Rule Making (NPRM) that DHS had promulgated for the implementation of Real ID specified the machine readable portion to consist of a PDF417 2D barcode. The NPRM, being the period in which interested parties and the public could comment, was an opportunity for Jim Harper of the Cato Institute to highlight the fact that there is a race field in the format specified by DHS. The specified format DHS proposed in the NPRM is the 2005 American Association of Motor Vehicle Administrators (AAMVA) Driver's License/ Identification Card Design Specification, Annex D (Harper, 2007).

Critics of the Act suggest that there is rarely a data field which specified in some standard which remains empty of data. Harper notes that DHS does not require all of the fields to be developed and populated in the standard, and certainly doesn't specify that the race field be developed – but also that "DHS has done nothing to prevent or even discourage the placement of race and ethnicity in the machine-readable zones of this national ID card." (Harper, 2007, p. 212) Mr.

Harper was adamant in his objection to the inclusion of a race field, urging DHS to mandate that the field not be used, stating (Harper, 2007, p. 212):

> Avoiding race- and ethnicity- based identification systems is an essential bulwark of protection for civil liberties, given our always-uncertain future. In Nazi Germany, in apartheid South Africa and in the recent genocide in Rwanda, horrible deeds were administered using identification cards that included information about religion, about tribe, and about race. Implementation of the REAL ID Act, which would permit race to be a part of the national identification scheme, would be a grave error. (Harper, 2007, p. 212)

In the final rules, DHS responded to concerns about the race field being included and possibly used – but did not specifically indicate that the race field was not to be used. In the response to a comment regarding the use of a race field in the final specification, DHS wrote

> Race is not a data element contemplated in this rulemaking and the reference in the NPRM to the AAMVA standard was not intended to include race as a data element in the MRZ for REAL ID. (Minimum Standards, 2008, p. 5305):

However, the next paragraph states:

> The final rule sets the minimum standards to include, but recognizes the authority of the individual States to add other elements such as biometrics, which some currently include in their cards. (p. 5305):

This is not a repudiation of the inclusion of a race field. In the response to the next comment, DHS again attempts to downplay the data element of race, without specifically prohibiting the states from using that field, stating:

DHS disagrees with the notion that the standard selected should be rejected because it includes coding for race. DHS has never stated that race should be encoded on the license, and specifically stated in the proposed rule that it was not incorporating wholesale the card data elements currently required by the AAMVA. (p.5305)

According to the specification, at D.12.3.2, the Race field (k), Data Element DCL, the race field is already an optional element. All of the fields in D.12.3.2 are optional, as the "required" fields are listed in Section D.12.3.1, "Minimum mandatory data elements." ("Personal Identification," 2005), so the last sentence in the final rules is questionable either in its accuracy or pertinence. If DHS, which mandates every part of the Real ID implementation, down to the exact date of each step of compliance, were to state that the race field would not be used, it would not be used. The rules specify what documents to accept, how and how long they are to be stored, what the machine readable zone will incorporate, what databases individuals' identities will be verified against and what type of photograph to use. If the Department of Homeland Security mandated that the race field was to not be used, it would not be used.

Alternatively:

...white people would carry the designation "W"; black people would carry the designation "BK"; people of Hispanic origin would be designated "H"; Asian or Pacific Islanders would be "AP"; and Alaskan or American Indians would be "AI." (*Real ID Act Hearings*, 2007, p. 175)

By not prohibiting its use, it is left to the individual states to use that field and it will be part of the MRZ for all citizens of whatever states elect to use it, if not tomorrow then the next day.

The 2D Barcode and its Security

Randy Vanderhoof, Executive Director of the Smart Card Alliance, an industry trade group which, among other activities, organizes the trade shows, such as the annual Smart Cards in Government Conference, wrote to express disappointment in DHS's choice of a 2D bar code, i.e. the PDF417 specification, during the NPRM phase of the rulemaking process. He wrote of the proposed specification

> This is where the document and DHS recommendation fall short. The core reason for the REAL ID legislation in the first place was supposed to improve security, not the least expensive solution for storage and transmission of data on which states could agree. (Vanderhoof, 2007, para. 2):

A glance at the *Standards for U.S. License Technology* table underscores the point – as 44 states and the District of Columbia are using 2D bar code technology. The states that are not are California, Michigan, New Mexico, Ohio, Texas and Wyoming ("Standards - U.S. License Technology," 2008). An interesting aside is that Wyoming is the home state of former Vice-President Dick Cheney, and that is the only state that uses no magnetic stripe, 1D or 2D bar code technology.

As a leader in the industry, the Executive Director of the SmartCard Alliance also writes that DHS in the NPRM phase of rulemaking did not address the issues of tampering, counterfeiting or duplication of documents for a fraudulent purpose, even though the opening summary of the proposed rules stated that these issues would be addressed (Vanderhoof, 2007). In the final rule, in Section 37.15, DHS pushes the responsibility for these action items off onto the states, with the caveat that the states must provide DHS with written reports specifying the manner in which these goals will be met. At the same time, the regulation specifies that the information will be considered SSI, or Sensitive Security Information, which "must be handled and protected in accordance with 49 CFR part 1520" achieved (Minimum Standards, 2008, pp. 5334-5335)

Therefore security and anti-tampering information falls under the purview of the Transportation Security Administration (TSA), as Title 49 is Transportation in the Code of Federal Regulations, and two important effects are immediately felt. Only persons with a "need to know" will receive the information (1520.11) and there is no release of the information under the Freedom of Information Act (1520.15 (g))

("49 C.F.R. Part 1520," 2004) This puts the information as to how the Real ID's are to be safeguarded against tampering outside the possibility of any type of independent review by members of the public, industry or academia. It also means that those who know what the safeguards are supposed to be, even if they find those safeguards deficient, cannot take the information to the public and force a security solution through publicity.

It is sometimes argued that "security through obscurity" is useful. Security expert Eugene Spafford, Ph.D., director of the Center for Education and Research in Information Assurance and Security (CERIAS) and an Association of Computing Machinery (ACM) Fellow (Cooper, 2001), has written on the subject and has come to the conclusion that "security through obscurity" does not work (Spafford, 2008). This is also the prevailing view in the computer security industry. Security through obscurity may work for awhile, and depending on the importance of the data and determination or lack thereof of the adversary, it may work indefinitely. (Think of the case of some obscure custom computer program written for a small office which runs on a computer not connected to a network and compare that to security for a database (or distributed database) holding millions of credit card numbers, or better yet, names, dates of birth and permanent addresses.) If the target is of value, attackers will attempt to compromise the security of the system.

Once the system has been compromised, the motivation of the entity compromising the security of the system must then be examined. This motivation will dictate how widely the knowledge of the exploit will be disseminated. The security of the system, once breached, then depends on how widely the knowledge of the vulnerability and exploit is disseminated. Some attackers may want to keep the exploit to themselves, assuring repeated success as they would cover their tracks and the breach may not be discovered. In the case of Real IDs, success would be measured by forging Real IDs and/or modifying the database(s). Some attackers may publish their discoveries of security vulnerabilities, allowing for wholesale compromise of the security of the system. In the meantime, secrecy on the part of the targeted system's administrators regarding the insecurities of the system will adversely affect the public. This would mean that every citizen of the

North American Union who live in states that are part of the Driver's License Agreement (DLA) would have their information at risk.

There exists at least one inconsistency between the Real ID specification which DHS published in its final rules and the format as the PDF417 standard is written, as well as inconsistency within the format. One inconsistency has to do with the use of the null data elements for unknown or unavailable data. In the FAQs on the AAMVA site for the format, the question has to do with the reading of paragraph D.12.3, which states that for optional data elements were the information is not available, "NONE" should be inserted into the field and for mandatory data elements, "unavail" should be recorded in that data field. The question concerned the situation in which the field is shorter than the null identification element, possibly causing the shortened 'N," "NO," or "NON," or "u," "un," "una," "unav," "unava," or "unavai" to be mistaken for some other code ("AAMVA Card," 2008). The FAQ answer indicates that the matter is under study. This diverges from the DHS rule which states in Section 37.17 (a) that if an individual has only one name, the single name should be placed in the "last name or family name" field, leaving the first and middle name fields blank. The rules specifically prohibit the use of "place holders" such as "NFN, NMN and NA." (Minimum Standards, 2008, p. 5335) In this case the DHS rules do not match the AAMVA PDF417 standard.

Bruce Schneier, a well-renowned security expert in the information security field and an expert who comments on all matter of security issues, testified in the May 2007 hearing before the Senate Judiciary Committee. In his statement to the committee he pointed out several problems with the security of Real ID. He noted that the ID could be no more secure than the documents used to procure the trusted ID. This meant that if a terrorist or criminal could not bribe a DMV clerk, the bad guy would try to forge source documentation or bribe a clerk at some agency which would produce the source documents for the ID. (*Real ID Act Hearings*, 2007)

Schneier testified to the committee that other problems could result from the existence of shadow databases. These databases would be written to by commercial entities every time the Real ID would be used in a commercial context, just as driver's licenses are now. Schneier brought up the case of lost Real IDs. With the knowledge that 20% of all identity documents are lost per year, he warned that any parallel or separate system for re-issuing lost IDs would also be susceptible to abuse. Another issue is that of a terrorist or criminal impersonating a law-abiding citizen. In this case, the question of the identity documents is similar, and in that instance the terrorist or criminal would be able access more easily the restricted spaces that the use of Real ID was supposed to protect. The poignant observation from Bruce Schneier: "And if you think it's bad for a criminal to impersonate you to your bank, just wait until a terrorist impersonates you to TSA." (*Real ID Act Hearings*, 2007, p. 237)

The more trusted a form of identification, the greater access the identification gives. Those who would forge an ID will be able to access more and better information and physical spaces when they forge a more trusted ID. In the United Kingdom, a country in which national identification cards have been issued and databases centralized, there is debate over the wisdom and efficacy of issuing national ID cards. A report from the London School of Economics takes issue with the British government's assertions and assumptions regarding the national ID. The report indicated that as ID's become more secure, those who would break the security and forge cards are becoming more resourceful (Rotenberg, 2006):

> Even as the cards are promised to more secure, attacks become much more sophisticated. Most recently, Russian security agents arrested policemen and civilians suspected of forging Kremlin security passes that guaranteed entrance to President Vladimir Putin's offices. (Rotenberg, 2006, p. 128)

The purpose of Real ID is to be the most trusted ID and DHS envisions that it will be used for employment verification, and for all of the uses driver's licenses are used for now. With the convenience of bar code, for now, and possibly RFID in the future, it will be used for all manner of transaction. Even as the government attempts to anticipate forgery and forgers, as Bruce Schneier explained in testimony before the Senate Judiciary Committee, the new twenty dollar bill was forged before it even hit the streets (*Real ID Act Hearings*, 2007, p. 234) With this being the case, and with the large numbers of ID cards which would have to be replaced when enemies forge Real IDs, there has to be acceptance of the fact that the criminals and terrorists with the most resources will be most able to breach the security of the Real IDs. And if this is the case, then the purpose of the Real ID cannot be for preventing terrorism, except of the lowest level and most casual kind. The people who will be using valid Real IDs will be law abiding citizens, and they will be the individuals that the nationwide surveillance system will track.

Computers, Databases and Security

One of the most intrusive and disturbing aspects of the implementation of the Real ID Act is the requirement that all states' databases be searchable by every other state and the federal government. This creates a situation which is more insecure than creating a large centralized database in terms of safeguarding the data. Yet it has the level of intrusiveness of a national ID database in that the data is all in one place (logically or virtually, as opposed to physically) by virtue of the ability to search distributed databases from multiple entry points. In computer parlance, to say it is logically in one place means that according to the computer's logical instructions, it matters not if all of the information is physically in one computer system located in one sub-basement or spread across the globe. The computer's logic, with the connections that the computers make with each other, and the speed of access and the speed with which the data can be moved from one computer to another, has the net result that the database is one "logical" entity. Just as the university computer and the Yahoo computer and are not in the same place, when accessing them from your home computer if you didn't know that, you might think that they were.

Almost everyone in contemporary society has an idea of what a computer is and what it can do. Computers are good at doing the same thing over and over, as opposed to doing something unique each time computing power is called upon to do something.

A database system can be thought of as a computerized record-keeping system. The foundational building block in the construction of a database is a "record." A record is a set of data, of which an example would be the set of data stored in the 2D barcode mandated in the rules for Real ID. When it becomes necessary to organize these records, they are stored in a database (Date, 1995).

Records have structures defined by the database designer(s), and each of these groups of records with the same structure is stored in a "table." A database can have many tables, and data fields in some tables may provide the links to other tables. These other tables may have records with different structures and may be filtered and sorted in different ways than the original table, but have information taken from the other tables (Date, 1995). In the example of Real ID, and the state DMV databases that make up the foundation for the distributed database, each record would be keyed to an individual. The key field in a record is a unique identifier and is the field which is used for access to the stored records. There are occasions when a key is composed of primary and other secondary fields, but for all intents and purposes, the operation of the database should be transparent to the end user. In other words, when the policeman or the coat check girl scans your Real ID, they don't need to know how the database is designed, or that the local database they are creating of their encounter with you is first checking a statewide database for your information. Then the database in your home state (assuming those are different) can be used to initiate queries to marketing databases and then whatever watch list databases the FBI or CIA or other member agency of the intelligence community dictate must be checked. The end users only just know that when they scan the machine readable zone of your national ID card that your picture and date of birth and home address and quite possibly race come up and they know it is you (according to the computer) who they are stopping randomly or to whom they are giving your coat.

For purposes of each state's database, it is hoped that each individual will have a unique driver's license or ID number (or alphanumeric identifier). After your time and location have been logged into these multiple databases so NSA can run an algorithm against your movements to see if you are doing terrorist things, you might be able to go on your way. Then again, if you are traveling over the same ground a criminal or terrorist traveled, in the same order, you might have some explaining to do – to the computer at the police station.

As each new individual is assigned a driver's license number, the data is entered and a number of record-keeping functions occur. The mechanics vary between implementations, and this is where the real world meets the world of computer science. The idea of the Real ID act is to produce a system in which each individual would have only one driver's license or ID card, regardless of state of issuance, at a time. Various mechanisms are to be employed, including checking against a database of Social Security numbers, various immigration databases, a system which is not up yet with vital events (such as births and deaths), etc. The trick for normalizing the data has to do with names, numbers associated with birth certificates in various jurisdictions, and the data in these other databases. Informally, normalizing the data refers to the process of combining or discarding, depending on the desired result, information from duplicate entries in databases in well-defined ways (Date, 1995).

Once the data is in the database, stored in fields that are organized into records in tables, users are going to want to query the database. Generally, Structured Query Language (SQL) is used. Also, users with the correct privileges and access rights to a database can change or input data. When one table has a field in a record which is changed, it is useful to have other tables with the same fields, whatever the record and table format, change also so that the data is consistent.

A relational database management system (RDBMS) updates all of the associated tables when a field that appears in more than one table changes. The term relational refers to the fact that data fields in certain tables relate to similar data fields in other tables.

Modern RDBMSs have graphical front-ends, so that users can construct queries without too much trouble. For the average user of the Real ID database system, however, the swipe of the 2D barcode will automatically query the database. The mechanism should be such that the state with which the Real ID is registered will be first to be queried.

For more advanced users, who want to correlate data from the card swipe with other data either from that database or others, the query capabilities would be much enhanced. In the commercial world, data aggregators such as Axciom, ChoicePoint and LexisNexis use extensively correlated databases such that they can query across several sources of information and find intersections, quickly and easily (Behar, 2004).

Then there is Seisint. Even back in the day, pre-9/11, correlative power of commercial databases was well-developed. O'Harrow (2005) tells the story of Hank Asher discovering the power of the database technology he helped build. Two days after 9/11, Asher was at his house with Bill Shrewsbury, a special agent with the Florida Department of Law Enforcement socially, when it struck him to see if he could profile the terrorists using the tools he had at his disposal. He narrowed the list of suspicious, according to the data, characters to 419 before he called a friend of his, Tim Moore, commissioner of the Florida Department of Law Enforcement (O'Harrow, 2005).

Ultimately, he produced a list 1,200 people who looked interesting. Five of those were evildoers who crashed airplanes into the World Trade Center. This number was achieved after knowing the attack had occurred, and this analysis produced a 99+% false positive rate (Jonas & Harper, 2006). So in this case, it was not predictive data mining, but data mining in hindsight. Nonetheless, law enforcement was very interested and for weeks afterward, law enforcement accessed Mr. Asher's databases at no charge.

At the end of the process, DHS envisions a system in which each person in the real world is associated with only one identifier in the computer's database, so that all the vital information about that person can be linked to in other databases, or, depending on the semantics, linked to in the relational database management system (RDBMS). The idea of constructing a network of databases, a distributed database, in which the information could be accessed quickly, is the foundation for Acxiom's business model. One of John Poindexter's aides at the Total Information Awareness Office wrote that, "Ultimately, the U.S. may need huge databases of commercial transactions that cover the world or certain areas outside the U.S. Acxiom could build this mega-scale database" (O'Harrow, 2005, p. 61). Acxiom officially suggested a different approach so as not to alarm the public, which was to "use networks to link those data systems together" (O'Harrow, 2005, p. 61).

In terms of the massive distributed database that the Real ID Act would create, Bruce Schneier in his testimony to the Senate Judiciary Committee was being generous when he testified that, "Computer scientists don't know how to keep a database of this magnitude secure." (*Real ID Act Hearings*, 2007, pp. 235-236) The fact is that computer scientists are struggling to come up with a theoretical model for keeping a computer secure, let alone a network. There are issues that range from the inherent insecurity of the underlying operating systems and the network protocols they use to communicate over a network, to the fallible humans that maintain and access the data the computers store. Even the Air Force admits that in 2005, systems were compromised, allowing hackers to make off with the data on over 37,000 Air Force personnel (Elliott, 2010).

Unauthorized access can mean many things. At the minimum it can mean individuals who have access to the system and data for specific purposes, looking at data that at which they are not supposed to look. An example of this type of unauthorized access would be an IRS employee, with legitimate access to the system storing tax returns, looking up the tax returns of celebrities when there was no legitimate job-related reason to do so, as John Snyder was convicted of doing (Coombes, 2008).

Unauthorized access can also mean some actor or organization gaining access when the system security was set up to stop those actors or organizations from accessing the system or data. Examples of this type of unauthorized access can be found in the description of any database breach, an example of which would be the TJX data breach in which at least 45.7 million credit and debit card numbers were stolen (Abelson, 2007).

Data breaches in commercial, educational and government databases, and other losses of data are in the news constantly. In the years from 2005 and 2009, between 250 million and 500 million records containing personally identifiable information (PII) of U.S. residents have been stolen from government and corporate databases. In 2009, some of the bigger breaches that were reported included 236,000 records from UNC Chapel Hill from a hacked server and 131,000 records from a stolen Army National Guard laptop. And on May 4, 2009, the Virginia Department of Health Professions reported over 8,000,000 records stolen by an extortionist hacker ("2009 Security Breaches," n.d.). It is patently absurd to think that somehow the data in the database(s) that the Real ID Act mandates would somehow be more secure. If anything, the data will be much less secure, due to the pressures on the administrators to keep their data available, and the distributed nature of access.

As the director of the Center for Education and Research in Information Assurance and Security (CERIAS) said in 1989, "The only truly secure system is one that is powered off, cast in a block of concrete and sealed in a lead-lined room with armed guards – and even then I have my doubts." (Spafford, 2006) Not much has changed since then to give the industry hope that things are more secure. Events have indicated that more systems have more valuable information to steal and are breached on a regular basis.

The news provides examples of breaches which underscore the enormity of the problem of keeping information secure. The Privacy Rights Clearinghouse maintains a database of database breaches, which is kept by. By their count, from January 2005 through October 24, 2010, the number of records containing personally identifiable information that has been exposed is 510,715,685 records from 1804 reported database breaches ("A Chronology of Data Breaches," 2010).

States' Resistance

Several states have resisted the imposition of the Real ID Act and its provisions on their procedures and processes for issuing driver's licenses. This resistance has taken various forms.

For example, Missouri adopted House Concurrent Resolution Number 20, which stated that the due to the insecurity inherent in the implementation and the threat of theft of data from the cards and elsewhere, that "...these potential breaches in privacy that could result directly from compliance with the REAL ID Act may violate the right to privacy secured in the Missouri Constitution..."and therefore the state of Missouri called on the Congress to repeal the Real ID Act ("Senate Committee Substitute," 2007).

Missouri State Representative Jim Guest sponsored a bill which would have made Missouri actively non-compliant with the Real ID Act in Missouri's 94th General Assembly ("House Bill No. 1716," 2008). The bill specified, among other provisions directly challenging the Real ID Act's specifications:

The department of revenue shall not amend procedures for applying for a driver's license or identification card in order to comply with the goals or standards of the federal Real ID Act of 2005, any rules or regulations promulgated under the authority granted in such act, or any requirements adopted by the American Association of Motor Vehicle Administrators for furtherance of the Act. (Section 3)

The bill never made onto the calendar for passage in that Missouri congressional session ("HB 1716," 2008).

Representative Guest and others felt that the Real ID Act was an infringement on privacy and appealed to the original values of the Founders. Representative Guest said, "We're supposed to be a government of, by and for the people. Government's role is to protect citizens' freedom. In this case they're not doing that. [The Real ID Act] is a direct frontal assault on the freedom of citizens when [the U.S. government] wants us to carry a national ID" (Ferguson, 2007b, p. 16).

In 2009, the Missouri legislature tried again and passed HB 361 which was signed into law by Governor Jeremiah W. (Jay) Nixon (D) on July 13, 2009. The law took effect on August 28, 2009 and mandated that the Department of Revenue not modify its driver's license procedures to comply with the Real ID Act. The law calls for the retrieval and deletion of biometric data gathered for the purpose of complying with the federal Real ID Act. It does not call for the deletion or removal of data gathered for other purposes, so conceivably there could still be biometric data held by the State of Missouri and/or its agencies. Presumably this information would not be available, however, in the distributed database mandated by the Real ID Act ("HB 361," 2009).

Another example of resistance involves the state of Montana. In January of 2008, Montana Governor Brian Schweitzer (D) wrote a letter to DHS saying that Montana was not complying with the Act and had no intention of doing so. He urged the governors of 17 states that had given indications of resisting the federal government's Real ID mandate to join with Montana and force a showdown regarding the May 11 deadline DHS had set for compliance or for states to apply for a waiver (Schweitzer, 2008). Georgia was one of the states which had been strongly opposed to the Real ID rules.

DHS spokesperson Laura Keehner was nonplussed when the possibility that all the Georgians traveling through Atlanta-Hartsfield airport, the United States' busiest airport, would have to go through secondary screening. "That will mean real consequences for their citizens starting in May if their leadership chooses not to comply. That includes getting on an airplane, so they will need to get passports." (Singel, 2008a)

The issue of states resisting DHS's Real ID-mandated requirements also stems partly from the fact that there had been cooperation between the state and federal government in attempting to set rules for driver's license issuance prior to passage of the Real ID Act. Governor Schweitzer specifically took umbrage to the fact that with the passage of the Real ID Act; the rule-making was unilaterally and precipitously given over to DHS. The Governor urged in his letter that states rally around the passage of S. 717 and H.R. 1117, acts which would reinstate "a negotiated rulemaking process that was on track to improve ID security." (Schweitzer, 2008) He sent that letter to the governors of Colorado, Georgia, Idaho, Maine, New Hampshire, Oklahoma, South Carolina, Arizona, Hawaii, Illinois, Missouri, Nebraska, North Dakota, Pennsylvania, Tennessee and Washington (Singel, 2008a).

S.717 in the 110th Congress was referred to Committee on Homeland Security and Governmental Affairs Subcommittee on Oversight of Government Management, the Federal Workforce, and the District of Columbia on April 29, 2008. Hearings were held but the bill never made it out of committee ("S. 717 [110th]", 2008) H.R. 1117 in the 110th Congress was sent to the House Oversight and Government Reform Committee and referred to the Subcommittee on Government Management, Organization, and Procurement on Mar 23, 2007. The bill never made it out of committee ("H.R. 1117 [110th]", 2008).

In March of 2008, it was revealed that DHS granted a waiver to Montana, in essence stating that Montana's governor's letter was tantamount to a request for a waiver (an extension in the time to comply with the Act.) Governor Schweitzer said in reply, "I sent them a horse and if they want to call it a zebra, that's up to them. They can call it whatever they want, and it wasn't a love letter." Additionally, on the issue of how the government was going to keep the information secure in this distributed database, the governor said, "They tell us it's safe. Tell that to the passport people." (Singel, 2008b) The reference to the "passport people" involved unauthorized access to passport information perpetrated by contractors at the State Department. These contractors were accessing the passport information databases for information regarding past travel of political candidates (K. C. Jones, 2008). Presumably there were fewer people authorized to view the passport database information than would be authorized to access the Real ID database collection, so the conclusion that Governor Schweitzer was drawing was that if an entity comparatively small such as the State Department could not guarantee the safety of the data in the passport control database, how could anyone assume that the data held in the Real ID database would be safe from unauthorized access?

Replying to the governor through the press, Assistant Homeland Security Secretary Stewart Baker said, "We're not in the business of asking states to say Uncle. We're in the business of trying to improve driver's license security" ("States Challenge Homeland Security's ID Deadline," 2008)

Governor Schweitzer objected to DHS's flip rhetoric in his letter. The Governor wrote:

> Secretary Chertoff's remarks yesterday [January 17, 2008], albeit about WHTI, not Real ID, reflect DHS continued disrespect for the serious and legitimate concerns of our citizens. I take great offense at this notion we should all simply "grow up." (Schweitzer, 2008, para. 6)

Secretary Chertoff was also dismissive of skeptics as demonstrated by this statement at the final rules press conference in response to a question about putting so much trust in a single piece of identification, saying, "...under that theory we should eliminate passports and let people come across the border using a note written by their third-grade teacher." (Chertoff, 2008b, para. 84)

At the same press conference Secretary Chertoff basically described the driver's license itself as useless for identification purposes. According to Secretary Chertoff, if a state did not adhere to the new Real ID specification it would "...send a message to people that basically says a driver's license is useless, it has no identification value, and it's the kind of thing you can pick up at, like, an amusement park when you pay a few bucks and they do some kind of funny identification." (Chertoff, 2008b, para. 75) Governor Schweitzer, made the point that Montana driver's licenses were already more secure than the Real ID Act standard specifies, and in a more timely manner. The Governor said, "We already have an ID system they are hoping to get to in seven years." (Singel, 2008b)

Elected officials in other states have expressed misgivings about Real ID. The Idaho Senate in March 2007 passed Joint Memorial 3, after the House had unanimously passed it, which was a resolution to refuse to comply with the Real ID Act. Governor Mark Sanford of South Carolina urged his legislators to resist compliance, noting that it would cost the state $25 million to comply initially, and an extra $11 million per year thereafter (Zalud, 2007)

Some states were headed in the direction of compliance with the Real ID Act. According to Secretary Chertoff, at the time the final rules were released, 40 percent of individuals lived in states which were starting to come into compliance with the Real ID Act (Chertoff, 2008b). Some states have gone further, issuing an identity instrument commonly known as the Enhanced Driver's License (EDL). Vermont is one such state that started issuing these IDs starting in early 2009 ("Applying," 2010; "Vermont Issues," 2009).

The EDL is said to ease the cross-border movement of individuals under the terms of the Western Hemisphere Travel Initiative (WHTI). Starting in 2008, United States citizens who traveled to Canada or Mexico needed passports or some type of WHTI compliant document to have crossed the border back into the United States. The states of Vermont, Washington, New York and Michigan had worked with DHS to enhance the security of their driver's licenses ("Overview," n.d.) and as of October, 2010, those four states issue Enhanced Driver's Licenses ("WHTI," n.d.).

These Enhanced Driver's License and identification cards (EDL/IDs) contain RFID chips, similar to the chips contained in U.S. passports. Holders of these enhanced driver's licenses can produce them when needing to produce a WHTI-compliant document, or government-issued photo ID and proof of citizenship to cross the border (K.C. Jones, 2007b).

Originally, the states in the vanguard of producing EDLs included Arizona. ("Proposed 'Enhanced' Licenses," 2007). The Governor of Arizona, Janet Napolitano, signed a law, HB 2677, which prohibits Arizona from complying with the Real ID Act ("HR 2677," n.d.). That bill passed the Arizona House March 19, 2008, passed the Arizona Senate May 6, 2008, and was signed into law on June 17, 2008 ("National ID," 2010). Governor Napolitano wrote, when she signed the bill, "My support of the REAL ID Act is, and has always been, contingent upon adequate federal funding. Absent that, the REAL ID Act becomes just another unfunded federal mandate." ("AILA InfoNet," 2008, para. 3)

Janet Napolitano was subsequently named Secretary of DHS in the Obama administration and sworn in on January 21, 2009 ("Secretary Janet Napolitano," 2009). In this role she then became responsible for enforcing the mandated implementation.

Increased Scope of Use

Secretary Chertoff and other spokespersons for DHS have had it both ways in the rhetoric. There is an insistence by the department that it is for federal purposes, that it is a way to make people safer on airplanes and in nuclear power plants, and federal buildings. The idea being that if the person who the ID says is holding it has made it to the door of the conveyance or building, then it is ok for them to pass through that doorway. But it is not enough for a person to have the ID to pass through the doorway. Security personnel frisk the person anyway. They inventory and inspect the contents of the citizen/subject's purse, wallet, computer bag, and pants pockets. Security will conduct this search, if not by physically turning those items or pockets inside out, then with backscatter X-ray machines bathing everything in cancer-causing ionizing radiation. These machines look through fabric, plastic and paper, record the images and display those images for the guards to inspect. Simultaneously, there is insistence from the Department of Homeland Security that there will be other uses for the ID, probably employment verification for a start. So the question again becomes, how is the Real ID Act a measure to stop terrorism more than it is a measure to facilitate the tracking of law-abiding citizens in their daily lives?

Security experts, editorial writers, think tank operatives and others are saying that the Real ID will be used for more and other purposes beyond its stated purpose. Schneier in his testimony to the Senate Committee on the Judiciary (2007) raised the issue of the commercial databases which will add Real ID-culled information and spring up around Real ID information. Thousands of bars and casinos use a card scanner to acquire information on their customers. One New Jersey night club, KatManDu, by 2006, had built a database of 15,000 customers and had the patrons' name, address, height, weight, eye and hair color ("Bars, Casinos," 2006). So every time the Real ID is swiped, which will be often, the information will end in many places. In many cases, the rhetoric of DHS is an attempt to turn these ancillary uses of citizens' private information into selling points for adoption. Jim Harper, of the Cato Institute, agreed with and quoted Anne Collins, Registrar of Motor Vehicles for the State of Massachusetts, as she predicted that uses of the Real ID card will go far beyond the Congressional intent. In the words of Ms. Collins as reported to the Senate Committee on the Judiciary (2007), "If you build it they will come" (p. 174).

To see a parallel endpoint which may be of some concern, one can look to China. They have the usual surveillance camera apparatus, 20,000 initially for the city of Shenzen, with computerized software to direct the cameras, and a facial recognition backend to track who is out on the street. (Klein, 2008)

China's residency cards, issued to residents starting in August 2007, contain a chip which stores information, such as the citizen's name, address, ethnicity/race, work history, police record, medical insurance information and status, landlord's phone number, educational background and reproductive status. In the future, credit histories, subway travel balances and petty cash allotments will be added. In the manner of a student ID card at a major university, the users will be able to make small purchases with these national ID cards. Michael Lin of Public Security Technology, the company that makes the cards, said,

"If they do not get the permanent card, they cannot live here, they cannot get government benefits, and that is a way for the government to control the population in the future."(Bradsher, 2007)

Some predict for the Real ID card, such trivial (compared to safeguarding airplanes from terrorists) uses as keeping track of "club membership, employment, library usage, even health and credit information." (Healey, 2008)

Possible Role of RFID in Future Real ID Implementations

RFID has applications across a variety of products. For tracking uses, RFID has the advantage of holding enough information that each item can have a unique identifier (Strickland & Hunt, 2005). That means that when an RFID tag is read, and it is correlated with the owner of the item tagged, the association can be made between the person and that RFID chip. Whenever the tag is read, the date, time and location of that encounter can be logged into a database. If an individual has multiple items with RFID tags, the tags can be associated with an individual and each other with high degree of certainty. These encounters can then be used to track the individual's movements. The individual could be identified by identifying the tags in any subset of the items the person owns (Albrecht & McIntyre, 2006).

There is also the concern that there will be a requirement to tag humans with RFID. Chips have been implanted in pets and livestock for years. The company CityWatcher.com, a video surveillance company in Cincinnati requires, as a condition of employment for workers in their security data center, that they have an RFID chip implanted in their bodies (Williams, 2007)..

A Wisconsin law banning forced implantation of RFID chips in people took effect in June 2006 (Songini, 2006). North Dakota passed a similar law in 2007.(Songini, 2007). The California Senate passed a bill in 2007 banning employers from requiring that employees have chips implanted. The law was to go into effect January 1, 2008 ("California RFID Bill Signed Into Law Today By Governor," 2007; del Barco, 2008).

CHAPTER 5:

The Real ID Act: Threat to Freedom

The Real ID Act in its currently envisioned form is a threat to privacy and freedom in American society. The cost-benefit ratio in the implementation of the act, even in a perfect implementation under the current rules, is poor and is outweighed by the good the money spent on implementation. More effective surveillance might consist of surveillance of individuals who were indicated by other intelligence to possibly be terrorists, as opposed to surveillance of all American citizens on the chance that one of them might turn into a terrorist.

The current rules themselves indicate the construction of a flawed implementation of the Act. Even if DHS mandated a more secure implementation, the insecurities inherent in the sprawling computer system the web of databases represents, would be impossible to implement securely. And a less than perfect implementation of a more secure specification would still be insecure.

Adding to the problems of this type of system is the panoply of threats that are faced by all computer networks and database systems. These include malware of all types, unauthorized access and insider abuse.

Insecurities in the Current Implementation

The information on the cards can be read by any 2D barcode scanner. These types of scanners will be employed in all manner of business to read the cards as they are presented and populate innumerable databases, each operated by some type of commercial entity. These commercial databases are a separate problem from the security at the state level of the driver's license issuing agencies.

There is no encryption mandated to protect the data on the cards. There is a mandate that DHS will certify states' IT systems as to the security of the data that gets queried with an authorized use of the card.

This is a specious guarantee as there is no oversight or third-party security review, so the public is to trust the federal government as it audits the states' IT systems. Every year the Government Accountability Office (GAO) audits IT security compliance of federal agencies every year and every year the results are bad. It would be safe to assume that the states are less adept than the at securing their systems.

The Problem of Privacy in a Surveillance Society

The problem of privacy of information about oneself as an American citizen is a problem which can be broken down into two parts. The first has to do with what information the government should be entitled to under the theory of security, and the second has to do with what information commercial interests should be allowed to store, maintain and sell. This includes contentless data such as where an individual is at any given time, or what they are wearing, as well as data with content, such as what an individual says, and to whom they say it.

The second question involves enumerated rights. Speech and assembly are enumerated rights, and it was assumed that in American society, one could travel to speak and assemble. The questions of freedom of assembly and anonymous association are directly tied to tracking technologies, such as inference tracking as it applies to phone calls, emails and Internet traffic.

To reclaim some sense of privacy of information as the situation iscurrently constituted may be futile. There is a vast amount of data held in private hands, and much money is being made from the sale and transfer of the information. What may be of some use is attempting to reclaim some of the enumerated rights.

Free market advocates might maintain that the best way to keep a company from buying and selling transaction information would be for consumers to not do business with companies that have lax or non-existent privacy policies. Froomkin (2000) advises that individuals not fill out surveys and warranty cards, and that they limit the amount of personal information they hand over to commercial entities when possible (p.1464). However, the inertial effect of the market that exists, and the amount of money involved in the data trade make it unlikely that any wholesale change in the way corporations buy, sell and handle data can be expected to materialize in the direction of more privacy for individuals in the manner in which their data is bought or sold by corporations.

We've Got the Wrong Guy

Getting the wrong guy is something that authorities are generally loathe to have to admit. There are numerous examples of individuals under the traditional criminal justice construct who are convicted of crimes they didn't commit. These errors, or "miscarriages of justice," occurred in the framework of a criminal justice system under which the Fourth Amendment and other procedural safeguards existed, and judicial oversight was accepted as having been exercised. Miranda rights, prohibitions against torture of suspects, due process protections, open courts, an appeals system; these are all constructions assumed to be in place on these occasions in which justice has been misapplied or miscarried.

In the world of secret courts with secret evidence and predictive data mining to identify those who might be terrorists in the future, intuitively, the implications are fairly serious in cases in which data is misapplied or the wrong individual is flagged for scrutiny. Without the Constitutional protections afforded by the rule of law and with secrecy implied, any mistakes will probably never be identified nor rectified.

It is easy to hypothesize examples in which the wrong individual could be implicated by remote tracking surveillance. Consider a crime where the neighbor's teenager had a copy of the victim's car key. The teenager has this key from a time when he ran an errand for the family and had the key copied. The teenager drives late at night with his friends to a deserted place near a power plant to use drugs and drink. Let's suppose that the victim's work cell phone had been left in the car. The tracking computer will see the personal phones at the car owner's house, but all the other tracking surveillance markers will indicate that the worker was nefariously casing the power plant. These markers would include highway RFID readers identifying the RFID chips in the car's tires along the highway, the OnStar records of GPS positioning, and the work cell phone location tracking records. If anything untoward were to happen at the plant, which is considered critical infrastructure by definition, and even possibly if not, that joyride might bring the police to the victim's house. At that point, the victim would hope that the teenager had brought a cell phone on that ride also.

Similar situations could occur due to the confluence of external events with the misidentified person talking to the "wrong" person, surfing to the wrong Web site, ordering the wrong thing, going to the wrong series of strip malls in a certain order (let's say that the malls have a rocketry store, a store with chemistry sets, and a UPS Store). If one watched the "wrong" shows on television or read the "wrong" books, one might come under increased scrutiny. Most of the time, there would be little follow-up. Ideally, the national security apparatus would verify that the person was not a threat to the government and then leave them alone.

During the manhunt for the D.C. sniper, Hank Asher used his Matrix system to attempt to identify the sniper based on the victims' residences, attempting to find some commonality to tie the murders together to help solve the crime. Asher rejected the government's theory that the sniper was, and tried his own theory, figuring the sniper had geographical ties to the area. By using his Matrix system, Asher came up with the name of a man:

> "So I ran a profile of the distance of every one of the murders, and I came up with a guy that lived like a hundred feet from one of them, five hundred feet from another, two thousand feet from another. I mean, the glove fit," he [Asher] said. "And I sent that up to them [law enforcement] and I can't imagine what that poor fellow..."

> "Hopefully he was cleared easily with alibis and excuses," he said. "But I thought I had caught him." (O'Harrow, 2005, p. 118)

There have been situations in which NSA passed along useless intelligence to the FBI. Specifically mentioned as the phone contacts of potential terrorists were phone numbers of babysitters and local pizza parlors. These numbers were passed from the NSA to the FBI. One FBI official said, "After you get a thousand numbers and not one is turning up anything, you get some frustration." (Bamford, 2008, p. 267) Diverting resources in this manner, to following up leads of dubious quality based on the mere fact of a phone call having been made, is a poor use of resources if the goal is anti-terrorism.

Obvious problems arise from the misidentification and misclassification of American citizens in these national security and law enforcement databases. O'Harrow relates the story of Stephan Nash and the Denver police. Mr. Nash was active in an organization named CopWatch, which attempted to expose police brutality and lawlessness of the police with regard to dealings with minorities in the city of Denver. He was also an activist in other legitimate political organizations. It was only through an insider passing on information to Nash and the ACLU that the domestic spying activities of the Denver police came to light.

The Denver police had been spying on civilians for years and the records were paper-based. In 2000, the city wanted to upgrade to computerized databases, and contracted with Orion Scientific, a company that took software developed by the Defense Advanced Research Projects Agency (DARPA) and extended it for use by domestic intelligence agencies.

What the city of Denver did not do was invest in training. Supervisors were allowed to make up the rules for categorizing the subjects of surveillance as the data was entered. The easiest category to put many of the spied upon was "criminal extremist." Mr. Nash and his wife were so labeled, as well as an elderly nun who worked with the poor Indians in Chipas and a Colorado University professor who spoke at a rally against police brutality (O'Harrow, 2005)

These actual and potential abuses are minimized by law enforcement, policy makers and the media as an adjunct of the government. The current reportage treats privacy abuses as unusual, portraying these as man bites dog stories. The prevailing frame is always, "If it saves even one life, then it is worth it." In acquiescing to the government's declaration of extraordinary powers and suspension of habeas corpus in general and for American citizens as "enemy combatants" ("Jose Padilla," n.d.; Levy, 2003) and allowing the creation of a separate legal system ("ACLU: Military Commissions Act of 2006," n.d.; "Military Commissions Act of 2006," 2006), citizens have demonstrated acceptance of this abuse. American society has moved away from the Founding Fathers' guiding principle of jurisprudence, which is credited to William Blackstone, which is that of "innocent until proven guilty." In the famous quote, "Better that ten guilty persons escape than that one innocent suffer" (Blackstone, 1893, p. 358; Volokh, 1997, p. 174) is found the abhorrence of arbitrary detention and show trials with rigged verdicts that the American Revolutionaries rejected in their bid for freedom from the King and his functionaries' whims and fairness in the legal process. The lack of substantive debate in the mainstream media and the framing of mainstream media coverage regarding this radical shift in American public policy in the legal realm is consistent with the Propaganda Model as advanced by Herman and Chomsky (1988).

Abuse of Trust

The scenario that hackers and thieves prefer is that of having everything they'd like to steal in to be found in one place. The Real ID distributed database will contain all of the data on all law-abiding American and citizens of participating states in the North American Union and therefore be that one repository for all the information the data thieves would like to steal. Sometimes the miscreants are seemingly trusted individuals. The three letter agencies also seem to have trouble identifying who might be a security risk and who is not a risk.

Nada Nadim Prouty, 37, who started life in Lebanon, was a former employee of the FBI and Central Intelligence Agency (CIA.) In November, 2007, she pleaded guilty to conspiracy to defraud the U.S. government. She allegedly fraudulently acquired U.S. citizenship, and then is said to have used her position at the FBI to access data about family members who are alleged to have connections to Hezbollah.

Prouty entered the U.S. from Lebanon in June 1989 on a non-immigrant student visa, stayed past the expiration of her visa, and then paid a U.S. to marry her, and on August 9, 1990, she was married. In April 1999, she was hired as a special agent of the FBI, was granted a security clearance and worked out of the Washington field office investigating crimes against U.S. persons overseas.

In August 2000, Prouty's sister married Talal Khalil Chahine, who is now a fugitive hiding out in Lebanon, according to DOJ. Chahine is wanted in connection with tax evasion in the matter of a concealed $20 million, some of which was diverted to Lebanon.

In June 2003, before leaving the FBI to join the CIA, she accessed the FBI's Automated Case System and queried her name, her sister's name, and that of Chahine. She resigned the CIA in November 2007 and offered to help the CIA on matters involving national security (Gross, 2007).

Two conclusions can be drawn from this affair. The first being that an organization which supposedly excelled at screening their applicants ended up letting an individual with questionable ties join. Once in the organization, an individual like Prouty was able to access sensitive information. The implication for the Real ID data is that in organizations with less rigorous screening, such as police departments, there is a greater likelihood that people who should not be trusted with American citizens' data will be. The second component involves the inherent insecurity of the data to insider abuse in general.

Abuse of Power

An audit of a mere 10 percent of the FBI's national security investigations from 2002 through 2007 revealed that the FBI had violated the law or agency rules on more than 1,000 occasions. The sample size and the numbers indicate that the FBI had illegally collected information several thousand times. The majority of the incidents involved phone companies and Internet Service Providers (ISPs) furnishing information the agents were not authorized to collect (J. Solomon, 2007).

A report issued in March of 2007 by the Justice Department did not uncover the extent of the illegality revealed in later in June of 2007, but did include Attorney General Gonzalez and FBI Director Robert S. Mueller admitting that the FBI broke the law in collecting information improperly under the PATRIOT Act. The Attorney General even left the door open to the possibility of pursuing criminal charges against FBI agents and lawyers who broke the law (Jordan, 2007).

Years later, in 2010, FBI agents were required to take an exam on the bureau's policies. It appears that many FBI agents cheated on the exam and Director Mueller could not be sure how many had cheated. However, he said the cheating probably occurred because the agents lacked understanding about the procedures. An Assistant Director, Joseph Persichini, retired during the investigation. Director Mueller assured Congress that despite the cheating, the FBI is following the rules about seizing records without warrants (Goldman & Apuzzo, 2010).

The Director also did not appear to be as conversant with the rules as he maybe should have been. After testifying to Congress, he sent Senator Dick Durbin a note "clarifying" an answer regarding a question about procedures similar to those that the tests covered (Goldman & Apuzzo, 2010).

There are numerous instances of police and various others who have accessed law enforcement databases with citizens' personal data, in an unauthorized fashion ("If you have nothing to hide..." 2008). One instance involved Officer Thersa Shover of the DeKalb County Police Department accessing the Georgia Crime Information Center database, a database that is supposed to be classified, to get information on her ex-husband's girlfriend. She then created flyers with the ex-husband's girlfriend's picture and captions labeling her an adulteress, homewrecker, etc., and sent these to the woman's family, friends, past employer, et. al., with social networking information gained from the database. More astonishing was the fact that she was suspended and not charged criminally ("Officer Suspended," 2008).

Insecurity of Information

There are instances in which sensitive and even classified information is not secure. This augurs poorly for the security of the Real ID database.

One instance of sensitive information being exposed on the Web comes from the architects commissioned to design the U.S. Embassy in Baghdad. The architectural firm, Berger Devine Yaeger Inc. of Kansas

City, on their Web site, exposed the master drawings for the embassy in May, 2007. The embassy sits on 104 acres in Baghdad (K. C. Jones, 2007) and was dedicated in January, 2009 ("U.S. Dignitaries Dedicate New American Embassy in Baghdad," 2009).

The State Department asked the firm to remove the drawings from their site but a spokesman for the company said that anyone who was interested the embassy site could just look it up on Google Earth. Around that time, Al Jazeera had reported bombings of construction equipment and that construction personnel had been injured. Using the architectural site drawings and the Google Earth information, it would have been an easy job to match construction phases with the activity observed at the site (K. C. Jones, 2007).

There are problems securing data in what are supposed to be the most secure environments. In 2007, various problems surfaced at Los Alamos Nuclear Lab (LANL). In one instance, a scientist sent an unencrypted email over the open Internet containing "highly classified" data from the lab to the test site in Nevada. And in May, 2007, a senior staffer from LANL took a laptop with "government documents of a sensitive nature" to Ireland. That laptop's hard drive was not encrypted and was stolen from the staffer's hotel room (Barry, 2007).

Government is not the Solution, Government is the Problem

Data and privacy problems can be addressed generally, even though they cannot be completely solved. Some general solutions apply to data other than the type kept in the Real ID databases. For instance, data can be aggregated and anonymized. An example of this involves vehicle registrations. Vehicle registration information is kept precisely and made available in the aggregate to various industry and trade groups ("U.S. automobile registrations," 2001). In these types of cases, there is no compelling need to maintain and transmit data which would link individuals to the data elements in various databases to commercial and governmental entities. The data should be aggregated as a way to anonymize data.

Personally identifiable information (PII) should always be encrypted, whether in the database or if stored on the national ID card. The federal government has been moving toward whole disk encryption since the U.S. Department of Veterans' Affairs (VA) data loss affair (Fisher, 2007). The VA data breach exposed 250,000 veterans' PII (Pulliam, 2007). Every Web browser has encryption built in for credit card transactions, among others. There is a system of certificates so that entities can be verified as to their identity against the certificate authority's certificate. Some certificates use a cryptographic algorithm, MD-5, which has exhibited weakness, and which allows forgers to create fake certificates ("MD5 Weakness," 2008). The problems with MD-5 are solvable, in that certificate authorities (CAs) can use a more secure algorithm such as SHA-1 and therefore a fairly secure certificate implementation can be achieved. When vulnerabilities are discovered in SHA-1, then another more secure algorithm will have been developed.

States have been selling their citizens' personal data to data aggregators for years. An example of this practice is the state of Minnesota, which sold driver's license information to over 5,000 outside groups. Attorney General Mike Hatch noted that:

> The name, address, height, weight and driver's license number of every Minnesota driver can be accessed over the Internet by anyone willing to pay for it. If you don't think that's shocking, the threat is brought to you by state government. (Scheck, 2006, para. 3)

There are other ways that insiders can gain information to which they shouldn't have access. These situations involve database inquiries, in which database queries can be constructed to destroy privacy. This type of attack is well-known and there is active research in the computer science community into ways to guard against those types of series of database queries which would reveal information which should remain private.

Total Surveillance

The net effect of total surveillance serves to chill individual freedom and expression, thereby enforcing conformity and denying the benefits of participatory democracy. The Hawthorne effect was observed by

Elton Mayo at the Western Electric Hawthorne plant in Illinois in a series of experiments on worker productivity. Although Jones (1992) conducted a reexamination of the original study, it is still conventionally accepted that people behave differently when observed. Jeremy Bentham's Panopticon, which revolutionized architectural and organizational design of prisons, factories, schools and orphanages, was based on the idea that control could be achieved by watching those who were to be controlled without the observed knowing whether or not they were being observed. This tended to make the subject population believe they were under surveillance at all times. Froomkin (2000) describes this effect in passing as a privacy issue. Strub (1989) takes this theme further, reading Orwell's 1984 through Bentham. As Strub wrote before most people could have known the power of the surveillance technology that would be unleashed on contemporary society, it is absolutely true at the time that he wrote that no Panopticon had ever been built (in its purest form), and that the theory of the Panopticon had not been applied in "real life." Strub notes, "...it is of interest that only in Orwell's novel has the theory been so completely realized..." (p. 40). Interestingly, Bentham had the idea that every item, every article should be recorded as a supplement to visual surveillance, as when the written record was examined, some item or other might prove important (Strub, 1989). And married with the total surveillance came the idea in 1984 that the thought criminal might dodge punishment for awhile, maybe years, but that the Thought Police would eventually catch the miscreant and punish that individual (Orwell, 1961).

The FBI and law enforcement agencies are now free to infiltrate peaceful social justice and groups expressing legitimate political dissent. This was the essence of COINTELPRO. The chilling effect of suppression of citizens' voices in the political process is inevitable under these circumstances (Carrie Johnson, 2008; Madigan, 2008). When people are deprived of their enumerated right of anonymity of association, people will not join and support causes that align with their policy and political views. That was the point of Justice Douglass' opinion in Laird v. Tatum. People act differently and make decisions differently when they are being watched. In Bamford's (2008) discussion of the Aquaint computer he notes, "Such a system would have an enormous chilling effect on everyone's everyday activities--what will the Aquaint computer think if I buy this book..." (p. 327). And that is the point.

In Mexico, legitimate political figures are wiretapped and surveilled by their own government. Guanajuato state governor Vicente Fox, later president of Mexico, had his phones tapped. An opposition Senator had seven years of his life recorded in wiretaps and physical surveillance (Bamford, 2008). "The system the Bush administration wanted for Mexico was similar to its warrantless eavesdropping operation in the U.S." (Bamford, 2008, p. 227)

In the United States, the Pennsylvania Department of Homeland Security spied on, Berks Peace Community, a group of Quaker-affiliated senior citizens who met regularly to hold a prayer vigil against the wars. Homeland Security was tipped by a firm that was under contract to the state, the Institute of Terrorism Research and Response (ITRR) who also monitored tweets (Edwards, 2010).

When a person has to think twice before saying something because unseen monitors are listening; when a person is afraid to buy a book because they might get flagged in a database as a terrorist; when a person is afraid to go get a cup of coffee at a coffee shop because musicians might be singing about something not perfectly aligned with government policy (folk singer Victor Jara was rounded up in 1973 in Santiago, Chile, shot in the hands and then shot 44 times for his political philosophy expressed in song in Chile (Klein, 2007)); one could say that these people live in a repressive society. What has been described are the hallmarks of totalitarian societies along the lines of East Germany and the Soviet Union in the past, or China today. Generally, the description reserved for total surveillance regimes is to describe these as Orwellian (Strub, 1989).

There are those who expound the virtues of conducting surveillance against all of the citizens all of the time. There are advantages associated with total surveillance. Crime might be reduced significantly. Missing people would not be missing for long. If the controllers of the surveillance apparatus decided, there would be no illegal alien in the country. The municipality and the state would be able to collect for every car as no citizen drive unregistered car for long within the surveillance perimeter. With RFID tagging of every object, there would be no object for which an accounting could not be made (Albrecht & McIntyre, 2006). No copyrighted work would be used without the proper royalties being credited. Children would always eat the mandated amount of food and schoolchildren would never let any of the allowed books fall into overdue status when checked out from the library. And of course, the purpose given for the total surveillance regime would hopefully be achieved, in that non-state terrorists would never be able to plot their evil deeds, nor carry them out, or when they did, they and their associates would be hunted down expeditiously.

There is the mistaken impression that the average citizen has little to fear because the government is awash in data and cannot possibly process all of the data on every citizen all of the time. Even if that were the case, the government is moving to solve that problem by beefing up the "fusion" centers and in at least one case, constructing a facility the size of the Alamo Dome for processing the data that the government admits it is collecting all of the time (Bamford, 2008). When someone makes the "wrong" move and gets put on a list, the all-seeing eye of the state will then be trained on that individual.

A 20-year old student, a U.S. born American citizen, Yasar Afifi, had a friend who posted something on a blog wondering why bad guys weren't more effective if there really were bad guys. This occurred soon after the Ninth District Court of Appeals ruled that law enforcement needs no warrant to track individuals using GPS on the subjects' vehicles. Mr. Afifi found a GPS device that had been planted by the FBI on his vehicle. He knew this because when he discovered the device and removed it, FBI and police showed up to demand he return their expensive piece of equipment, the Orion Guardian ST820, produced by Cobham. Only law enforcement can buy this model. A retired FBI agent said that the new models don't have batteries. Batteries run out and need to be replaced. The preferable method is now to get power directly from the subject's car battery (Zetter, 2010).

No Need to Disrobe – We'll Save You the Trouble

The No-Fly List is a perfect example of what can happen to someone when they get on the wrong list. The "No-Fly List" and "Selectee List" had a million names between them representing approximately 400,000 people (obviously each terrorist has on average 2.5 names) (Pincus, 2009). Many Americans are on that list when they should not be. Naomi Wolf (2007) contends that one use of the list is a way to inconvenience individuals who disagree with administration policies (p. 95). She hypothesizes that that is why she is on the list. Others on the list cannot even remotely be considered a terrorist threat to aviation by being on the plane. A United States Senator, Ted Kennedy, was on the list when he was alive, and he also had disagreed with the Bush Administration's policies (Wolf, 2007). The singer Cat Stevens, who changed his name to Yusuf Islam when he converted to Islam, was on the No-Fly List. He managed to get onto the London to Washington, D.C. flight on his way to the recording studio in Nashville. His plane was diverted to Bangor, Maine, then after questioning he went to Boston and then Washington, D.C. before being sent back to London, on a plane. Cat Stevens sings about peace. Secretary of DHS at the time Tom Ridge said that Cat Stevens was "one of my favorite artists." ("'Amused' Cat Stevens," 2004, para. 21)

Meanwhile, "Catherine Stevens has been questioned because her name in its diminutive matches that of the singer formerly known as Cat Stevens." (Sharkey, 2006, para. 3) At the time, Senator Ted Stevens was on the committee that regulates the airlines and asked Kip Hawley, the head of TSA at the time, "How do people get off these lists?" The occasion was Mr. Hawley's testimony before the Senate Commerce Committee. (Sharkey, 2006)

Cat Stevens subsequently demonstrated the fallibility of the "No-Fly" List by "clearing" his name when he released an album ("Cat Stevens back," 2006). He appeared at a political rally on the National Mall in Washington, D.C. in 2010 ("Ozzy Osbourne," 2010).

The TSA counters that, if Ted Kennedy were alive in 2010, he would not have been on the No-Fly list, and that he was actually only mistaken for being on the "Selectee List." ("Myth Buster," n.d.) The Selectee List, is a list of people who are "automatically and intentionally selected for enhanced screening every time they fly." ("Frequently Asked Questions About the No-Fly List," 2005, para. 2)

The "TSA Myth Buster" site is an interesting exercise; however it appears to be inaccurate. An 8-year-old boy is on the Selectee List and can't get off of it. He couldn't get checked in at the kiosk when he was a baby. TSA patted him down the first time when he was two. His mother, Najlah Feanny Hicks explains the procedure as it stands now, "Up your arms, down your arms, up your crotch — someone is patting your 8-year-old down like he's a criminal." (Alvarez, 2010, para. 8) This frisking occurred in prior to the new frisking rules that allow TSA to go beyond what had been previously thought to be the bounds of decency (Handy, 2010).

The "Christmas bomber" (aka "underwear bomber") was on the Terror Watch List, which has fewer individuals on it than the No-Fly list, but somehow mysteriously not on the No-Fly list. And this individual was escorted onto an airplane bound for Detroit in 2009. He had purchased a ticket with cash, had no luggage and no identification. So the question becomes one of why was this person allowed to fly when the average American has to have a Real ID-compliant ID to fly?

In other cases, the power of databases over people's lives when a mistake is made can be considerable. In some of the cases of "mistaken identity," there is no recourse for the party who was harmed. O'Harrow (2005) relates the story of the widow of a senior Postal Service executive. She was born to the son of a slave, and as a child in the South, for her safety, she recalls that she was forced to take cover on the floor of her father's business because angry, menacing gunmen were upset at the fact that black aviators were allowed to fly in combat in World War II. Routinely, repeatedly, the TSA would make the same "mistake." Every time she flew, she was detained until minutes before her flight. Then she would have to run to make the flight. Repeated letter writing and other attempts at remedies did not help. She carried a letter from the FBI saying she was not a terrorist. TSA workers ignored the FBI letter and she was told there was no recourse in that she would never get off the list (pp. 230-231). Since that time, the TSA has instituted a policy whereby an American citizen would have to apply for and be approved for a "redress number." This is an additional identifier that the citizen must use to identify him/herself to the "authorities."

To obtain a "redress number," the subject must go to the DHS Traveler Redress Inquiry Program (TRIP) web site and check all of the applicable scenarios which they've experienced. Some of these include, "I was told my fingerprints were incorrect or of poor quality," "I am always subjected to additional screening when going through an airport security checkpoint," "The airline ticket agent stated that I am on a Federal Government Watch List," and "I am directed to a ticket counter every time I fly."("DHS: Activities & Programs," n.d.)

For people "mistakenly" put on a list, a redress number is required under the TSA's policies instituted in mid-2009. When making a reservation, the subject is to "provide [his/her] full name, date of birth and gender as it is shown on the identification document you plan to present at airport security checkpoints. This information is not optional." ("TSA Secure Flight," 2009, para. 1)

This is in addition to the fact that passengers' luggage is searched; the passengers remove various articles of clothing including their shoes and belts, sweaters and jackets and are herded through metal detectors and patted down.

When the TSA started to allow citizens to obtain redress numbers, there were some teething pains. In October 2006, the TSA launched a web site for people to submit their information to get their redress numbers. The contract to create the site was no-bid. It was awarded by a TSA employee to Desyne Web Services of Herndon, Va., a company for which the TSA employee had previously worked. One of the data submission pages did not use encryption, and the encrypted pages were not properly certified. The person at TSA responsible for contract oversight was a friend, from high school, with an individual working for the contractor and the TSA contracting officer socialized with the owner of the contracting firm. Over 230 individuals submitted PII to DHS and were notified that their information had been at risk. No action was taken against the contractor or the contracting officer (Gradijan, 2008).

In 2008, the ultimate invasion of privacy and assault on dignity was imposed upon the American flying public. These airline customers are herded through "full body scanners." In the chambers of these machines, the passengers assume "poses" (basically they put their hands up as if they are under arrest) and are then irradiated with x-rays (backscatter) or scanned using terahertz wave electromagnetic radiation. These scans result in naked pictures of the passengers' bodies for airport security staff to peruse ("Which is it: Millimeter Wave or Backscatter?," 2008).The reportage on these scanner deployments popped up on the corporate media radar in October 2008 (O'Neill, 2008), the month before the 2008 Congressional and presidential elections and again in October 2010.

The first public relations challenge that faced the TSA was trying to fool the public into believing that the naked pictures did not show the genitals. Der Spiegel posted sample images of the quality one might expect from a representative machine. ("Check am Flughafen," 2008) TSA maintains that the sample images on their Web site are materially different than the Der Spiegel pictures and that the genitals were blurred using some sort of proprietary "privacy algorithm." ("Which is it," 2008) The comparison of the images of the naked bodies is probably a matter of taste or style and is left as an exercise for the reader. Jim Spellman, CNN's Department of Homeland Security's producer, account of the naked body scan that he underwent should be instructive. "She rotated the black and white 3-D image so I could see every contour of my body, including my private parts. I could see sweat under my arms, the rivets in my jeans and a pack of gum in my back pocket," he wrote (Spellman, 2008, para. 6)

Also, people will have to face the fact that members of the opposite sex will be looking at their naked pictures, as illustrated in a Mail Online article picture ("Airport body scanners," 2010) and as recounted by David Hammer, when he described that a female's naked body scan being viewed by a male TSA worker (Hammer, 2010).

Then the government said that the images were not stored and that there was no capability for the machines to store the images (Hammer, 2010). However, in August, 2010 the U.S. Marshall's service revealed that it had stored 35,314 naked pictures from just one checkpoint at a Florida courthouse (McCullagh, 2010). This is an expected result as the specification for the Whole Body Imager (WBI) devices in 3.1.1.3.1.2 calls for "exporting of image data in real-time," "provide a secure means for high-speed transfer of image data" and "allow exporting of image data (raw and reconstructed)." ("Procurement Specification," 2008) There is obviously a semantic game being played, again with the question of where data is stored. Based on the admissions by the U.S. Marshall's service, the images were stored somewhere. Based on a close reading of the specifications, the data could be transferred to some site other than the airport. Local storage capability would then be a liability, and the TSA could say (as they do) that the images are deleted 20 seconds after a passenger passes through the machine. (Sisk, 2010) And TSA could also say that, "the agency will have no ability to retain [the images]." (Hammer, 2010, para. 11) They would have simply transmitted the image to storage elsewhere.

In Britain, the government workers were forced to stop putting individuals under the age of 18 through the chambers, as the use of the machines was in violation of EU law. Specifically, the use of those machines was determined to be tantamount to manufacturing child porn (Scott Warren, 2010). Parents cannot give consent for the making of indecent pictures of their children (Zaba, 2010) Use of these scanners is the ultimate invasion of privacy of an adult and obviously a serious criminal offense when a child is subjected to this degradation.

The manufacturers and TSA obviously have an interest in minimizing any concerns regarding the safety of the radiation is used to produce images of the scan subjects. A team led by Boian Alexandrov in a physics journal, have modeled the damage that it appears terahertz waves cause to human DNA. This damage includes interference "...with processes such as gene expression and DNA replication." (KFC, 2009, para. 6) In this case, terahertz (THz) waves are shown to cause genetic damage. Or, as the writer for MIT's Technology Review put it, "That's a jaw dropping conclusion." (KFC, 2009, para. 6)

In the case of the backscatter X-rays, one can intuit that a pencil-thin x-ray being beamed at every square inch of your body is probably not the best thing for you. The government says it is perfectly safe (N. Savage, 2010). Dr. David Brenner, head of Columbia University's Center for Radiological Research is not so sanguine. Dr. Brenner notes that the skin is the most radiation-sensitive part of the body and therefore more susceptible to damage from X-rays than other tissues. He also says the dose of X-rays is likely 20 times more than originally claimed by the government and the manufacturers of these machines. Dr. Brenner notes that people have differing capabilities for repairing gene damage and that children and people with gene mutations (approximately one in 20 of the population) will be especially adversely affected by these machines. ("Airport body scanners," 2010)

The TSA installed 292 WBI machines into 61 airports in the time frame of March, 2010 through October, 2010 (Sisk, 2010), which brings the total number of machines to 341 in 67 airports with 110 more machines due to be installed by the end of 2010 (Kravitz, 2010).

For those who wish to avoid the humiliation of having their naked body inspected by strangers, there are other ways the government uses to take passengers out of their comfort zones. TSA has instituted new ways of searching passengers' bodies. "TSA agents will be allowed to touch body parts that were once off limits." (Holguin, 2010, para. 3)

"The way you used to pat down a passenger in the airport was with the back of the hands. Now we've switched it to the front of the hands. You go down the body, up to the breast portion, and if it's a female passenger, you're going to see if there's anything in the bra," said Charles Slepian of the Foreseeable Risk Analysis Center. (Holguin, 2010, para. 4)

TSA spokesperson Kristin Lee explained, "Passengers should continue to expect an unpredictable mix of security layers that include explosives trace detection, advanced imaging technology, canine teams, among others." (E. Sullivan, 2010, para. 6) By "others" we can intuit that she means, "being touched in places that were once off-limits."

By all accounts, the TSA workers are also not genteel in the way they treat those who would opt out of the full body scans. Sharkey reported that the TSA workers were rude to him when he asked to not be radiated and gave him a rough "pat-down" (Sharkey, 2010).

In the UK, refusal to submit to the naked body scan can result in the individual being barred from the flight. In March, 2010, two woman refused to submit and were barred from their flight to Islamabad, Pakistan (Tran, 2010). The House of Commons' Home Affairs Committee apparently has no sympathy for privacy concerns, saying, "Air passengers already tolerate a large invasion of their privacy and we do not feel that full body scanners add greatly to this situation. Privacy concerns should not prevent the deployment of scanners," ("Airport worker warned," 2010) So again, your family's naked pictures being taken and stored in a government database is not "adding greatly" to the already "large invasion of their privacy."

These machines are now used in other facilities beyond airports. As of October, 2010, there were approximately 13,000 scanning stations in use nationwide (Kravitz, 2010). One of these places is the courthouse in Denver, Colorado,

Now there are mobile units which rove the streets, using much more high-powered radiation. These machines are sold all over the world and are used in Iraq and Afghanistan, as well as being deployed by local law enforcement agencies in the U.S. These Z Backscatter Vans (ZBVs) can look into vehicles through the vehicles' exteriors, and also see through the walls of people's houses. The company that makes the radiation machines, American Science & Engineering (AS&E), won't say who the customers are in the United States, and neither is the government (Greenberg, 2010). So they could be driving down your street right now, blasting your house with radiation and looking through your clothes down to your skin.

Joe Reiss, the Vice President at AS&E, says that the even though the systems "to a large degree will penetrate clothing," that their machines don't have the level of detail when it comes to looking at people through their clothes that airport security scanners produce. Mostly they are just to see into cars and houses and only peripherally the people inside. Mr. Reiss continued, "From a privacy standpoint, I'm hard-pressed to see what the concern or objection could be." (Greenberg, 2010, para. 8) And Mr. Reiss assures his customers that the machines are able to store the images and information. "We do what our customers need." (Greenberg, 2010, para. 11)

Marc Rotenberg of the Electronic Privacy Information Center is attempting to remind the company, government "officials," and the public that there is still a Fourth Amendment, unless the extraordinary powers dictated by the PATRIOT Act and other "anti-terror" acts are invoked. The Fourth Amendment has to do with search and seizure, and that these devices, when deployed on the street, violate that Amendment of the Bill of Rights. (Greenberg, 2010)

And always, due to the invasive nature of these devices, and just as "sensitive" databases are accessed improperly, so too these devices are used in unauthorized fashion. In the UK, "The police have issued a warning for harassment against an airport worker after he allegedly took a photo of a female colleague as she went through a full-body scanner at Heathrow airport." (Tran, 2010) Note that in the U.K., the word choice was "photo" to describe the image produced by the WBI. The offending worker also allegedly made a lewd remark while the female coworker was in the body scanner chamber ("Airport worker warned," 2010)

And in the United States, the abusive nature of the paradigm was revealed when a TSA worker attacked his abusive co-worker over repeated abusive remarks about the size of his genitalia. The TSA workers apparently must pass through the scanners as part of their job. In May 2010, Rolando Negrin was arrested for aggravated battery for attacking his coworker with a baton. Mr. Negrin's co-worker had apparently been harassing Mr.Negrin for over a year regarding Mr. Negrin's physical attributes, and according to the police report, Mr. Negrin told the police he "could not take the jokes any more and lost his mind." ("Airport worker warned," 2010, para. 7)

There are always problems when that much power is wielded over defenseless people. Rebecca Solomon, 22, a University of Michigan student, was submitting to the searches at a checkpoint at the Philadelphia airport when the TSA worker reached into her bag and took out a bag of white powder that the TSA worker claimed he had found in the bag. She was reduced to tears trying to explain to this TSA worker that she had never seen the item before. "The worker 'waved the baggie at me and told me he was kidding, that I should've seen the look on my face.'" ("Student Pranked," 2010, para. 7) The best the TSA could do came from TSA spokesperson Suzanne Trevino, "The behavior exhibited by this TSA employee was highly inappropriate and unprofessional." ("Student Pranked," 2010, para. 12)

Sometimes the power goes to the TSA workers' heads in other ways. One TSA worker had gotten off his shift and was arrested at Terminal One at LAX, acting "erratically" and saying, "I am god, I'm in charge." (Baldonado & Weber, 2010) And after a TSA Internal Affairs investigation, one TSA drug user was fired (Baldonado & Weber, 2010, para. 1).

As the Real ID is used to track American citizens who have committed no crime, writing their daily activities into databases, there are more chances for an innocent person to do something that will trigger an investigation. There are more chances for "mistakes." As the processing power of the computers analyzing the data grows, more people will be flagged. And more "mistakes" will be made. The surveillance apparatus will be fed with data from the tracking of law-abiding American citizens swiping their insecure, unencrypted Real ID at the health club, the airport, the doctor's office, the library, the clothing store (to make sure they are who their credit card says they are) and the supermarket.

The Rhetoric of the Global War on Terror

The United States has set out in its long-term goals for combating terrorism; the ideal of "freedom and dignity that comes when human liberty is protected by effective democratic institutions" (*National Strategy for Combating Terrorism*, 2006, p. 1). Later in the strategy paper, the USA PATRIOT Act is held up as a reform that promotes security while "also protecting our fundamental liberties" (*National Strategy for Combating Terrorism*, p. 4). In the long-term approach section of the strategy for winning the war on terror, the long-term goal is stated as "Advancing effective democracy."

The rhetoric in the National Strategy for Combating Terrorism for fighting the Global War on Terror is replete with references to the concept of participatory democracy for other countries. "But elections are not enough. Effective democracies... are responsive to their citizens, submitting to the will of the people." (National Strategy for Combating Terrorism, 2006, p. 9) Yet the reality regarding the Real ID Act, which has been opposed by as many as 38 states at one time, indicates that the federal government will do what it will, regardless of the citizens' wishes.

The government attempted to make the case that Real ID would lead to greater security in cases of attempting to protect the public and the state from the truly bad people, the "evildoers" as President Bush characterizes them. The idea is flawed, but the implementation is further flawed. In the words of Bruce Schneier, it is "security theater" (Schneier, 2007a). And, as Schneier also noted in his testimony to the Senate, it is a "lousy security trade-off," which will cost at least $20 billion and the taxpayer "won't get much security in return." (*Real ID Act Hearings*, 2007, p. 237) Also, it must be assumed that knowledgeable people understand that this bit of security theater is not effective when the public isn't buying it. Yet there must be a reason that DHS and those who are pushing this idea are pushing so hard. There can only be two possibilities, or a combination of the two.

The first is the fact that there is so much money to be made. The second involves the secondary uses of the technology and the value of the information produced as a second order effect in the use of these technologies.

In understanding the believability of the rhetoric of DHS, one must consider that the agency pushing this on the American, Mexican and Canadian public, and then the world public, are the people who staged a fake news conference. FEMA (which is part of DHS) convened a "news conference" about the California wildfires that was carried on some cable channels. They announced the staged event 15 minutes before it was to start, and real reporters could dial in to listen but not ask questions. The individuals in the room who were asking the questions were FEMA employees posing as reporters. The day this fake event was staged was one of the last days on the job for the FEMA director of external affairs, John "Pat" Philbin. Mr. Philbin moved on to his new post as head of public affairs at the Office of the Director of National Intelligence (Hsu, 2007a).

Great Britain is in a similar situation vis-à-vis the Global War on Terror. Their country has been struck by terrorism, most notable was the attack on the London subway system. The British Intelligence-Led Policing model had been adopted by the United States. Law enforcement wants the surveillance abilities that Britain's national network of closed circuit TV cameras represents. Yet Sir Ken Macdonald, who was on his way out as Director of Public Prosecutions, made the statement that "the expansion of technology by the state into everyday life could create a world future generations 'can't bear.'" (Hope, 2008, para. 7) Sir Ken warned about the "Big Brother" state. He also warned Members of Parliament:

> It is in the nature of State power that decisions taken in the next few months and years about how the State may use these powers, and to what extent, are likely to be irreversible.

> They will be with us forever. And they in turn will be built upon. So we should take very great care to imagine the world

we are creating before we build it. We might end up living
with something we can't bear. (para. 15-16)

Bamford's (2008) book concludes with the following warning:

More than three decades ago, when the NSA posed a fraction
of the privacy threat it poses today with the Internet, digital
communications, and mass storage, Senator Frank Church, the
first chairman of the Senate Intelligence Committee,
investigated the NSA and issued a stark warning:

That capability at any time could be turned around on
the American people and no American would have
any privacy left, such [is] the capability to monitor
everything: telephone conversations, telegrams, it
doesn't matter. There would be no place to hide. If
this government ever became a tyranny, if a dictator
ever took charge in this country, the technological
capacity that the intelligence community has given
the government could enable it to impose total
tyranny, and there would be no way to fight back,
because the most careful effort to combine together
in resistance to the government, no matter how
privately it was done, is within the reach of the
government to know. Such is the capability of this
technology.

There is now the capacity to make tyranny total in
America. Only law ensures that we never fall into
that abyss--the abyss from which there is no return.
(pp. 344-345)

EPILOGUE

Winston and Julia Smith read some of the books listed in the reference section of this work. They paid with cash, understanding that before all money became electronic, it was their best bet to hope their book purchases would raise one less flag in the national database. After reading the books they knew that the RFID readers they were sure to have encountered in the store and on their way into and out of the store would transmit the data from all the RFID tags with which their belongings were tagged (Albrecht & McIntyre, 2006). One of those belongings was sure to have been bought with a credit card.

They knew also that if an investigator investigating the identities of individuals who might have purchased various books wanted photographic "evidence," that the digital camera feed, keyed to the bar code or RFID scanner entries for the book purchases, would give them away. The investigator could get the pictures, sound and cash register data without ever leaving his office at the Bureau of Freedom as it could be instantly accessed and sent over the Freedom Net (what had been previously called the Internet.)

The Smiths could have tried to borrow the books from the library. If the library had any copies of any of the books, the Smiths would have had to produce library cards and they would have been tied to the books that way. And their fingerprints would be in more places--on the pages of the books, "proof" that they read the books. The Smiths wondered if the video-conferencing capability on the HDTV was turned on for live surveillance, of if they were only being recorded. Not wanting to take a chance, they went into the bathroom and ran the water in the sink before they had a discussion. They may or may not have been aware that NSA had developed software to catch whispers (Bamford, 2008) and that there was software available that could separate out their speech from the background of the water running on analysis. They could write to each other on a piece of paper, and that would have probably been the best idea. Writing is time consuming but was the only reasonable attempt at a solution to the anti-surveillance problem. The Smiths would need to do so out of the field of view of the HDTV and not next to a window. If there were cameras installed at some point during a visit by DHS (or their contractors), that would also be a problem as the Smiths would not know where those cameras had been installed. And the Smiths would need to be wary of any flying insects that might have made their way into the abode, as those insects might well be camera equipped robots (Weiss, 2007). Even so, hidden cameras might have already been installed prior to their moving in. There was no way they could know.

Winston and Julia discussed possibly joining some type of privacy group online, but decided against it because that would raise another red flag in the national database. They discussed whether they should join a privacy or social action group that had actual meetings, but decided against it because they were afraid they might be put into the database as criminal extremists by government infiltrators. They debated writing a letter to the newspaper. Using their real names to complain to the media might trigger a red flag in the national database. Even if they used pseudonyms, the letter would have their fingerprints. Even if they wore gloves, the "secret" dots on the paper tying the the printed copy printer to the printed copy would give them away. They decided that anyway, based on what they knew from Herman and Chomsky, that the letter wouldn't be published anyway.

The Smiths understood that the surveillance state wasn't coming, it was there. They decided that their only option would be to do nothing and pray that they were safe for another day. They turned the water off and went back to sitting in front of the HDTV, so that they could be more easily watched.

REFERENCES

9/11_Commission. (2004). *The 9/11 Commission Report.* Washington, D.C.: 9/11 Commissiono. Document Number)

49 C.F.R. Part 1520 - Protection of Sensitive Security Information. (2004, May 18). *Code of Federal Regulations* Retrieved December 27, 2008, from http://law.justia.com/us/cfr/title49/49-9.1.3.4.7.html

2009 Security Breaches and Database Breaches. (n.d.). *IdentityTheft.info* Retrieved October 25, 2010, from http://www.identitytheft.info/breaches09.aspx

AAMVA Card Design Specifications: FAQs. (2008). *American Association of Motor Vehicle Administrators* Retrieved December 27, 2008, from http://www.aamva.org/KnowledgeCenter/Standards/Current/DLIDSpecificationFAQs.htm

Abdul-Alim, J. (2000, October 22). Racine Sailor Details Attack. *Milwaukee Journal Sentinel.* Retrieved October 5, 2008, from http://www.jsonline.com/news/metro/oct00/cole23102200a.asp

Abele, R. (2005). *A User's Guide to the USA Patriot Act and Beyond.* Lanham, Maryland: University Press of America, Inc.

Abelson, J. (2007). Breach of data at TJX called the biggest ever [Electronic Version]. *Boston Globe.* Retrieved August 27, from http://www.boston.com/business/globe/articles/2007/03/29/breach_of_data_at_tjx_is_called_the_biggest_ever/

About Smart Cards: Applications: Transportation. (2009). *Smart Card Alliance* Retrieved January 6, 2009, from http://www.smartcardalliance.org/pages/smart-cards-applications-transportation

About WikiLeaks. (n.d.). *WikiLeaks* Retrieved October 24, 2010, from http://www.wikileaks.org/media/about.html

ACLU: Military Commissions Act of 2006. (n.d.). *American Civil Liberties Union* Retrieved February 22, 2009, from http://www.aclu.org/safefree/detention/commissions.html

An Act Concerning Aliens, (1798).

AILA InfoNet Doc. No. 08070764. (2008, July 7). *American Immigration Lawyers Association* Retrieved October 25, 2010, from https://www.aila.org/content/default.aspx?bc=1019|25668|23276|235 74|25885

Airport body scanners 'could give you cancer', warns expert. (2010, June 30). *Mail Online* Retrieved October 31, 2010, from http://www.dailymail.co.uk/health/article-1290527/Airport-body-scanners-deliver-radiation-dose-20-times-higher-thought.html

Airport worker warned over body scanner 'harassment'. (2010, March 25). *CNN* Retrieved October 31, 2010, from http://edition.cnn.com /2010/WORLD/europe/03/25/uk.heathrow.scanner/index.html?eref=e dition

Albrecht, K., & McIntyre, L. (2006). *Spychips: how major corporations and government plan to track your every move.* New York: Penguin Group.

Alvarez, L. (2010, January 13). Meet Mikey, 8: U.S. Has Him on Watch List *New York Times* Retrieved November 1, 2010, from http://www.nytimes.com/2010/01/14/nyregion/14watchlist.html

'Amused' Cat Stevens back home. (2004, September 23). *CNN* Retrieved October 31, 2010, from http://edition.cnn.com/2004/US/09/23/ stevens.back.britain/

Applying for a New Vermont DMV Identification Card - DMV Guide. (2010). *The Unofficial DMV Guide* Retrieved October 25, 2010, from http://www.dmv.org/vt-vermont/id-cards.php

Avery, S. (2008). Patriot Act haunts Google service. Retrieved October 4, 2010, from http://www.theglobeandmail.com/servlet/story/ RTGAM.20080324.wrgoogle24/BNStory/Technology/?cid=al_gam_ nletter_dtechal

Badey, T. (1998). Defining International Terrorism: A Pragmatic Approach. *Terrorism and Political Violence, 10*(1), 90-107.

Baldonado, K., & Weber, S. (2010, January 7). TSA Agent Arrested at LAX. *NBC Los Angeles* Retrieved October 31, 2010, from http://www.nbclosangeles.com/news/local-beat/TSA-Security-Agent-Arrested-at-LAX-80858482.html

Bamford, J. (2008). *The Shadow Factory.* New York: Doubleday.

Bank Secrecy Act: FinCEN and IRS Need to Improve and Better Coordinate Compliance and Data Management Efforts. (2006).

Washington, D.C.: Government Accountability Officeo. Document Number)

Bar coded boarding passes. (n.d.). *International Air Transport Association* Retrieved October 31, 2010, from http://www.iata.org/whatwedo/stb/Documents/BCBP_english.pdf

Barrett, C. (2002). FBI Internet Surveillance: The need for a Natural Rights Application of the Fourth Amendment to Insure Internet Privacy. *Richmond Journal of Law and Technology, 8*(Spring).

Barry, J. (2007, June 25). Lax and Lazy at Los Alamos. *Newsweek* Retrieved October 16, 2010, from http://www.newsweek.com/2007/06/24/lax-and-lazy-at-los-alamos.html

Bars, Casinos Swipe Personal Information from Drivers License. (2006, November 22). *theNewspaper.com* Retrieved October 25, 2010, from http://www.thenewspaper.com/news/14/1457.asp

Behar, R. (2004, February 23). Never Heard of Acxiom? Chances are It's Heard of You. *Fortune* Retrieved November 7, 2008, from http://money.cnn.com/magazines/fortune/fortune_archive/2004/02/23/362182/index

Bennett, M. (1966). The Immigration and Nationality (McCarran-Walter) Act of 1952, as Amended to 1965. *The ANNALS of the American Academy of Political and Social Science, 367*(1).

Bhattacharya, I., & Getoor, L. (2007). Collective entity resolution in relational data. *ACM Transactions on Knowledge Discovery from Data (TKDD), 1*(1).

Big Bucks: Billions for Surveillance (2008, October 4). Retrieved February 15, 2009, from http://www.videosurveillanceguide.com/articles/big-bucks-billions-for-surveillance.htm

Biggs, B. S. (2001, April 13). Welcome to OnStar. How May We Invade You? *Mother Jones* Retrieved October 23, 2010, from http://motherjones.com/politics/2001/04/welcome-onstar-how-may-we-invade-you

Bill of Rights. (1791). Washington, D.C.: Library of Congress.

Binkley, C. (2004, November 22). Numbers Game: Taking Retailers'
Cues, Harrah's Taps Into Science of Gambling; Others Focus on High
Rollers While Casino Giant Prefers Telemarketing, Databases; From
East Chicago to Caesars. *Wall Street Journal* Retrieved January 9,
2009, from http://www2.lib.purdue.edu:2118/pqdweb?index=0&did=
740619091&SrchMode=2&sid=1&Fmt=3&VInst=PROD&VType=P
QD&RQT=309&VName=PQD&TS=1231555367&clientId=31343

Blackstone, W. (1893). BOOK THE FOURTH. Of Public Wrongs. In G.
Sharswood (Ed.), *Commentaries on the Laws of England in Four
Books. Notes selected from the editions of Archibold, Christian,
Coleridge, Chitty, Stewart, Kerr, and others, Barron Field's Analysis,
and Additional Notes, and a Life of the Author.* . Philadelphia: J.B.
Lippincott Co.

Bloss, W. (2008). Escalating U.S. Police Surveillance After 9/11: an
Examination of Causes and Effects. *Surveillance and Society, 4*(3),
208-228.

Bradsher, K. (2007, August 12). China Enacting High-Tech Plan To Track
People. *New York Times*, from http://www2.lib.purdue.edu:
6624/purdue?url_ver=Z39.88-2004&url_ctx_fmt=infofi/fmt:kev:
mtx:ctx&ctx_enc=info:ofi/enc:UTF-8&ctx_ver=Z39.88-
2004&rfr_id=info:sid/sfxit.com:azlist&sfx.ignore_date_threshold=1
&rft.object_id=110975413976006

Branum, T. (2001). *Aviation Security in the New Century*: Federalist
Society for Law & Public Policy Studieso. Document Number)

Bremmer, C. (2008, September 9). French revolt over Edvige: Nicolas
Sarkozy's Big Brother spy computer. *TimesOnline* Retrieved
December 31, 2008, from http://www.timesonline.co.uk/tol/news/
world/europe/article4703054.ece

Brownlee, N., & claffy, k. (2004). Internet Measurement. *Internet
Computing: IEEE, 8*(5), 30-33.

Burke, J. (2004). Al Qaeda. *Foreign Policy*(142), 18-20+22+24+26.

Bush, G. (2003, December 13, 2003). Statement on H.R. 2417. *Office of
the Press Secretary* Retrieved November 18, 2007, from
http://www.whitehouse.gov/news/releases/2003/12/20031213-3.html

Bush, G. (2005, May 11). President's Statement on H.R. 1268. Retrieved
December 19, 2008, from http://www.whitehouse.gov/news/
releases/2005/05/print/20050511-6.html

Bush, G. (2006, March 9, 2006). Statement on HR 199. *Office of the Secretary* Retrieved November 20, 2007, from http://www. whitehouse.gov/news/releases/2006/03/20060309-8.html

Bush, G. (2008, February 29). Executive Order: President's Intelligence Advisory Board and Intelligence Oversight Board. *The White House* Retrieved December 31, 2008, from http://www.whitehouse.gov/ news/releases/2008/02/20080229-5.html

Bush, G. W. (2001). Address to a Joint Session of Congress and the American People Retrieved November 17, 2008, from http:// www.whitehouse.gov/news/releases/2001/09/20010920-8.html

Caldwell, P. (2006). GPS Technology in Cellular Telephones: Does Florida's Constitutional Privacy Protect Against Electronic Locating Devices? *Journal of Technology Law & Policy, 11*(June).

California RFID Bill Signed Into Law Today By Governor. (2007). *ACLU of Northern California* Retrieved January 4, 2009, from http://www. aclunc.org/issues/technology/blog/california_rfid_bill_signed_into_la w_today_by_governor.shtml

Cangeloso, S. (2008, September 30). RFID tag anything with Tikitag. *Geeks.com* Retrieved January 11, 2009, from http://www.geek.com/ articles/chips/rfid-tag-anything-with-tikitag-20080930/

Carr, R. K. (1951). The Un-American Activities Committee. *The University of Chicago Law Review, 18*(3).

Case3:06-md-01791-VRW Document748. (2010, August 12). *United States District Court for the Northern District of California* Retrieved October 24, 2010, from http://www.eff.org/files/filenode /att/alharamainreply81210.pdf

Case M:06-cv-01791-VRW Document 639. (2009, June 3). *United States District Court for the Northern District of California* Retrieved October 24, 2010, from http://www.eff.org/files/filenode/ att/orderhepting6309_0.pdf

Case: 10-15616 ID: 7439555. (2010). *United States District Court for the Northern District of California* Retrieved October 24, 2010, from https://www.eff.org/files/filenode/jewel/Jewelopeningbrief9thCircuit. pdf

CaseM:06-cv-01791-VRW Document703. (2010). *United States District Court for the Northern District of California* Retrieved October 24, 2010, from https://www.eff.org/files/filenode/jewel/jeweldismissal 12110.pdf

CaseM:06-cv-01791-VRW Document721. (2010, March 31). *United States District Court for the Northern District of California* Retrieved October 24, 2010, from http://www.eff.org/files/filenode/ att/alharamainorder33110.pdf

Cassese, A. (2006). The Multifaceted Notion of Terrorism in International Law. *Journal of International Criminal Justice, 4*(5), 933-958.

Cat Stevens back on Peace Train ... sort of (2006, November 22). *MSNBC* Retrieved November 4, 2010, from http://today.msnbc. msn.com/id/15852711

The Cell Phone Challenge to Survey Research. (2006, May 15). *Pew Research Center* Retrieved January 11, 2009, from http://people-press.org/report/276/

Charny, B. (2004, September 29). Janet Jackson still holds TiVo title. Retrieved January 7, 2009, from http://news.cnet.com/Janet-Jackson-still-holds-TiVo-title/2100-1041_3-5388626.html

Check am Flughafen: Scannen bis auf die Haut. (2008, October 23). *Spiegel Online* Retrieved October 30, 2010, from http:// www.spiegel.de/fotostrecke/fotostrecke-36433-4.html

Chertoff, M. (2006a). Remarks by Secretary of Homeland Security Michael Chertoff on September 11: Five Years Later. Retrieved June 8, 2008, from http://www.dhs.gov/xnews/speeches/sp_ 1158335789871.shtm

Chertoff, M. (2006b, December 13, 2006). Remarks by Secretary of Homeland Security Michael Chertoff, Immigration and Customs Enforcement Assistant Secretary Julie Myers, and Federal Trade Commission Chairman Deborah Platt Majoras at a Press Conference on Operation Wagon Train. Retrieved April 24, 2008, from http://ww.dhs.gov/xnews/releases/pr_1166047951514.shtm

Chertoff, M. (2008a, January 16). Michael Chertoff: National ID security. Retrieved December 20, 2008, from http://www.sacbee.com/ opinion/v-print/story/636479.html

Chertoff, M. (2008b, January 11). Remarks by Homeland Security Secretary Michael Chertoff at a Press Conference on Real ID. Retrieved December 25, 2008, from http://www.dhs.gov/xnews /speeches/sp_1200320940276.shtm

Chomsky, N., & Matta, W. (2008, August 1). Untitled interview: Noam Chomsky interviewed by Wissam Matta, Assafir newspaper (Lebanon). Retrieved January 10, 2009, from www.chomsky .info/interviews/20080801.htm

A Chronology of Data Breaches. (2010, October 24). *Privacy Rights Clearinghouse* Retrieved October 25, 2010, from http://www. privacyrights.org/sites/default/files/static/Chronology-of-Data-Breaches_-_Privacy-Rights-Clearinghouse.pdf

Clerk's Notice in Al-Haramain Islamic Foundation, Inc. et. al. v. George W. Bush et. al. (2009, January 6). *United States District Court for the Northern District of California* Retrieved January 10, 2009, from http://www.eff.org/files/filenode/att/alharamaincmc010609.pdf

Cole, D., & Dempsey, J. (2002). *Terrorism and the Constitution.* New York: The New Press.

Cole, E. (2003). *Hiding in plain sight : steganography and the art of covert communication.* New York: Wiley Pub.

Comments of: Electronic Privacy Information Center (EPIC) and [Experts in Privacy and Technology]. (2007). *EPIC`* Retrieved October 23, 2010, from http://epic.org/privacy/id-cards/epic_realid_comments.pdf

Congressman Sensenbrenner. (n.d.). Retrieved December 21, 2008, from http://sensenbrenner.house.gov/Biography/

Coombes, A. (2008, August 20). IRS employee sentenced for snooping. *MarketWatch* Retrieved January 3, 2009, from http://www. marketwatch.com/news/story/irs-worker-snooped-tax-records/story.aspx?guid=%7B786BACBD-C58F-481B-AE31-28C2101E7CF6%7D

Cooper, G. (2001, February). ACM SIGSOFT SEN: ACM Fellow Eugene H. Spafford. *ACM SIGSOFT* Retrieved February 21, 2009, from http://www.sigsoft.org/SEN/spafford.html

Countryman, A. (2003, December 28). Illegal Insider Trading Detection
    Takes Digging, Sophisticated Surveillance. *Knight Ridder Tribune
    Business News* Retrieved January 9, 2009, from http://www2.lib.
    purdue.edu:2118/pqdweb?index=14&did=515929531&SrchMode=1
    &sid=2&Fmt=3&VInst=PROD&VType=PQD&RQT=309&VName
    =PQD&TS=1231555902&clientId=31343

Crenshaw, M. (2001). Why America? The Globalization of Civil War.
    Currrent History, 100(650), 425-432.

CS101 Card Swipe 2D Bar code Reader. (n.d.). *Alibaba.com* Retrieved
    November 1, 2010, from http://www.alibaba.com/product-
    gs/230838670/CS101_Card_Swipe_2D_Bar_code.html

Data Mining with MicroStrategy: Using the MicroStrategy BI Platform to
    Distribute Data Mining to the Masses. (n.d.). *Bitpipe* Retrieved
    October 16, 2010

Date, C. J. (1995). *An Introduction to Database Systems* (6th ed.). New
    York: Addison-Wesley Publishing Company, Inc.

Davis, D. W., & Silver, B. D. (2004). Civil Liberties vs. Security: Public
    Opinion in the Context of the Terrorist Attacks on America.
    American Journal of Political Science, 48(1), 28-46.

del Barco, M. (2008, January 1). California Law Outlaws RFID Implant
    Mandate. *National Public Radio* Retrieved February 29, 2009, from
    http://www.npr.org/templates/story/story.php?storyId=17762244

Deleting Web Browser Cookies & Cache. (2006, August 31). *New York
    University Information Technology Services* Retrieved January 7,
    2009, from http://www.nyu.edu/its/faq/cache.html

Devita-Raeburn, E. (2008). If There's Really Only Six Degrees (of
    Separation) Between Us and Osama bin Laden, Why Can't We Find
    Him? . *Discover, 29*(2), 42-46.

DHS Basic Pilot /E-Verify Program. (2008, March). *National Immigration
    Law Center* Retrieved February 21, 2009, from http://www.nilc.org
    /immsemplymnt/ircaempverif/e-verify_infobrief_2008-03-13.pdf

DHS: Activities & Programs | Area(s) of Concern. (n.d.). *Department of
    Homeland Security* Retrieved October 31, 2010, from https://
    trip.dhs.gov/

Digital recording with Dibos in bank applications. (2004, March 3). *Bosch* Retrieved January 9, 2009, from http://resource.boschsecurity.com/documents/DiBos19InchDigi_ApplicationReference_Bank_enUS_T2 822415627.pdf

Ditzion, R. (2004). Electronic Surveillance in the Internet Age: The Strange Case of Pen Registers. *American Criminal Law Review, 41*(Summer).

Dixon, R. (1997). Windows Nine-to-Five: Smyth v. Pillsbury and the Scope of an Employee s Right of Privacy in Employer Communications. *Virginia Journal of Law and Technology, 2*(Fall).

Doran, M. (2002). The Pragmatic Fanaticism of al Qaeda: An Anatomy of Extremism in Middle Eastern Politics. *Political Science Quarterly, 117*(2), 177-190.

The Drivers Privacy Protection Act (DPPA) and the Privacy of Your State Motor Vehicle Record. (n.d.). *Diogenes, LLC* Retrieved October 27, 2010, from http://www.diogenesllc.com/dppashort.html

Dunham, R. S. (2005). The Patriot Act: Business Balks [Electronic Version]. *Business Week.* Retrieved October 27, 2007, from http://www.businessweek.com/bwdaily/dnflash/nov2005/nf20051110_9709_db016.htm

E-Commerce Law Week, Issue 560. (2009, June 6). *Steptoe & Johnson, LLP* Retrieved October 25, 2010, from http://www.steptoe.com/publications-6165.html

E-Z Pass Toll System. (2006, January 18). *import rival* Retrieved January 7, 2009, from http://www.importrival.com/modules/AMS/article.php?storyid=37

Edwards, D. (2010, November 4). Pennsylvania Homeland Security monitored residents' tweets. *Raw Story* Retrieved November 5, 2010, from http://www.rawstory.com/rs/2010/11/pa-homeland-security-monitored-tweets/

EFF Analysis of 'Patriot II'. (n.d.). Retrieved November 18, 2007, from http://w2.eff.org/Censorship/Terrorism_militias/patriot-act-II-analysis.php

Eggen, D. (2006, January 28, 2006). 2003 Draft Legislation Covered Eavesdropping. *Washington Post.* Retrieved November 18, 2007, from http://www.washingtonpost.com/wp-dyn/content/article/2006/01/27/AR2006012701476.html

Elias, P. (2007, August 6). Secret call log at heart of wiretap challenge. *USA Today* Retrieved January 10, 2009, from http://www.usatoday. com/tech/news/surveillance/2007-08-05-thedocument_N.htm?csp=34

Elliott, D. (2010, October 25). Air Force manual describes shadowy cyberwar world. *Associated Press* Retrieved October 25, 2010, from http://news.yahoo.com/s/ap/20101025/ap_on_re_us/us_cyberwarfare _manual

Elmore, M. (2001). Big Brother Where Art Thou, Electronic Surveillance and the Internet: Carving Away Fourth Amendment Privacy Protections,. *Texas Tech Law Review, 32.*

Emergency Supplemental Appropriations Act for Defense, the Global War on Terror, and Tsunami Relief, 2005, (2005).

Eureste, M. A. (2008, December 18). Steps to Avoid Violating Employee Privacy Rights. *HR Tools* Retrieved January 9, 2009, from http:// www.hrtools.com/insights/mary_alice_eureste/steps_to_avoid_violati ng_employee_privacy_rights.aspx

Ezovski, G. M., & Watkins, S. E. (2007). The Electronic Passport and the Future of Government-Issued RFID-Based Identification. *Proceedings of IEEE International Conference on RFID, 2007,* 15-22.

Ferguson, R. B. (2007, February 28). DHS Confirms Real ID Act Regulations Coming; States Rebel. *eWeek* Retrieved October 19, 2008, from http://www.eweek.com/c/a/Mobile-and-Wireless/DHS-Confirms-Real-ID-Act-Regulations-Coming-States-Rebel/

Fisher, D. (2007, January 10). Federal government pushes full disk encryption. *Information Security Magazine* Retrieved November 5, 2010, from http://searchsecurity.techtarget.com/news/column/ 0,294698,sid14_gci1238490,00.html

Fishkin, K. P., Jiang, B., Philipose, M., & Roy, S. (2004, June). I Sense a Disturbance in the Force: Unobtrusive: Detection of Interactions with RFID-tagged Objects. *Ubicomp* Retrieved January 11, 2009, from http://www.seattle.intel-research.net/pubs/062420041544_244.pdf

Florida Constitution. (1968). *Florida Senate* Retrieved January 10, 2009, from http://www.flsenate.gov/Statutes/index.cfm?mode= constitution&submenu=3&tab=statutes&CFID=120535607&CFTOK EN=21785735#A01S23

Foley, J. (2007). Are Google Searches Private? An Originalist Interpretation of the Fourth Amendment in Online Communication Cases. *Berkeley Technology Law Journal, 22*(Annual Review).

Fox, B. (2006, April 26). Invention: Apple's all-seeing screen. Retrieved November 7, 2008, from http://www.newscientist.com/article.ns?id=dn9059&print=true

FR Doc E8-17123. (2008, July 25). *Federal Register* Retrieved October 23, 2010, from http://edocket.access.gpo.gov/2008/E8-17123.htm

Frederickson, S. (2008). Tapping into the reporter's notebook. *The News Media & the Law, 32*(4).

Freiwald, S. (2007). First Principles of Communications Privacy. *Stanford Technology Law Review, 2007.*

Frequently Asked Questions About the No-Fly List. (2005, September 22). *ACLU of Washington* Retrieved October 31, 2010, from http://www.aclu-wa.org/news/frequently-asked-questions-about-no-fly-list

Froomkin, A. (2000). The Death of Privacy? *Stanford Law Review.*

Gamage, D. (2010, October 16). United States Government blocks flow of independent funds to WikiLeaks. *Asian Tribune* Retrieved October 24, 2010, from http://www.asiantribune.com/news/2010/10/16/united-states-government-blocks-flow-independent-funds-wikileaks

Garfinkel, S. (2008, September 1). Information of the World, Unite. *Scientific American, 299,* 82-87.

Garrett, G. (1919). Free Speech and the Espionage Act. *Journal of the American Institute of Criminal Law and Criminology, 10*(1).

Garrow, D. (1988). FBI Political Harassment and FBI Historiography: Analyzing Informants and Measuring the Effects. *The Public Historian, 10*(4), 5-18.

Gast, P. (2010, September 24). FBI searches homes as part of terrorism probe. *CNN* Retrieved October 24, 2010, from http://edition.cnn.com/2010/CRIME/09/24/fbi.searches/index.html

German Consumers Rebel over RFID Tracking at METRO Future Store. (2004, February 26). *SpyChips* Retrieved January 11, 2009, from http://www.spychips.com/press-releases/german-protest.html

Glancy, D. (1995). Privacy And Intelligent Transportation Technology. *Santa Clara Computer and High Technology Law Journal, , 11.*

Glenn, M. (2003). *A Summary of DoS/DDoS Prevention, Monitoring and Mitigation Techniques in a Service Provider Environment*: SANS/GSECo. Document Number)

Godfrey, S. (2008, December 3). Nobody Rides for Free. *Washington City Paper* Retrieved February 22, 2009, from http://www.washingtoncitypaper.com/display.php?id=36563

Goldberg, M. (2005). The Googling Of Online Privacy: Gmail, Search-Engine Histories And The New Frontier Of Protecting Private Information On The Web. *Lewis and Clark Law Review, 9*(Spring).

Goldman, A., & Apuzzo, M. (2010, July 28). Putting the 'F' in FBI: Did agents cheat on tests? . *MSNBC* Retrieved November 3, 2010, from http://www.msnbc.msn.com/id/38446997/ns/politics/

Goodin, D. (2009, February 2). Passport RFIDs cloned wholesale by $250 eBay auction spree. *The Register* Retrieved February 3, 2009, from http://www.theregister.co.uk/2009/02/02/low_cost_rfid_cloner/

Goodman, A. (2008, September 4). Eight Members of RNC Activist Group Lodged with Terrorism Charges. *Democracy Now* Retrieved January 10, 2009, from http://www.democracynow.org/2008/9/4/ eight_members_of_rnc_activist_group

Goodman, A., & Klein, M. (2008, July 7). AT&T Whistleblower Urges Against Immunity for Telecoms in Bush Spy Program. *Democracy Now* Retrieved January 9, 2009, from http://i4.democracynow.org/2008/ 7/7/att_t_whistleblower_urges_against_immunity

Goodman, A., Rosa, E., German, M., & Clancy, E. (2008, August 1). Colorado "Fusion Center" to Step Up Intelligence Gathering During DNC; US Northern Command to Play Role. *Democracy Now* Retrieved January 11, 2009, from http://www.democracynow.org/ 2008/8/1/colorado_fusion_center_to_step_up

Goodman, A., & Weiser, W. (2006, October 31). Vote Suppression in 2006: Rule Changes Threaten to Disenfranchise Hundreds of Thousands of Eligible Voters. *Democracy Now* Retrieved January 9, 2009, from http://www.democracynow.org/2006/10/31/vote_ suppression_in_2006_rule_changes

Gorman, S. (2008, March 10). NSA's Domestic Spying Grows As Agency Sweeps Up Data *Wall Street Hournal* Retrieved October 31, 2010, from http://online.wsj.com/article/SB120511973377523845.html

Government Requests for Real Time Phone Location Data Divide Magistrates. (2006). *Electronic Commerce & Law Report, 11*(2).

GPS Vehicle Tracking Systems. (2008). *Enfotrace* Retrieved January 9, 2009, from http://www.enfotrace.com/market/index.html

Gradijan, D. (2008, January 14). Computerworld: Congressional Report Blasts TSA for Web Site Security Lapses. *CSO Magazine* Retrieved October 31, 2010, from http://www.csoonline.com/article/216957/computerworld-congressional-report-blasts-tsa-for-web-site-security-lapses

Graham, N. (2005). Note: Patriot Act II and Denaturalization: An Unconstitutional Attempt to Revive Stripping Americans of Their Ciittizenship. *Cleveland State Law Review, 52.*

Granger, S. (2001, December 18). Social Engineering Fundamentals, Part I: Hacker Tactics *Security Focus* Retrieved February 20, 2009, from http://www.securityfocus.com/infocus/1527

Greenberg, A. (2010, August 24). Full-Body Scan Technology Deployed in Street-Roving Vans. *Forbes* Retrieved October 30, 2010, from http://blogs.forbes.com/andygreenberg/2010/08/24/full-body-scan-technology-deployed-in-street-roving-vans/

Greene, T. (2004, October 14). Feds approve human RFID implants. *The Register* Retrieved January 10, 2009, from http://www.theregister.co.uk/2004/10/14/human_rfid_implants/print.html

Greenemeier. (2007, July 5). Downed Electronic Jihad Site Flew Under The Radar. *Information Week* Retrieved July 10, 2007, from http://www.informationweek.com/news/showArticle.jhtml?articleID=200900590

Grier, D. A. (2006). The Innovation Curve. *Computer, 39*(2), 8-10.

Gritzinger, B. (2008, September 26). Black box on board. *Auto Week* Retrieved January 8, 2009, from http://www.autoweek.com/apps/pbcs.dll/article?AID=/20080924/FREE/809189970/1023/THISWEEKSISSUE

Gross, G. (2007). Former FBI, CIA agent pleads guilty to computer crime [Electronic Version]. *ComputerWorld, 2008.* Retrieved November 13, 2007, from http://www.computerworld.com/action/article.do?command=printArticleBasic&articleId=9046802

H.R. 418 - THOMAS (Library of Congress). (2005). Retrieved
December 20, 2008, from http://thomas.loc.gov/cgi-
bin/bdquery/z?d109:HR00418:

H.R. 1117 [110th]: REAL ID Repeal and Identification Security
Enhancement Act of 2007 (2008). *GovTrack* Retrieved October 25,
2010, from http://www.govtrack.us/congress/bill.xpd?bill=h110-1117

Haas, B., & Giovis, J. (2008, May 20). Crime can strike fast at South
Florida malls. *TCPalm* Retrieved February 15, 2009, from
http://www.tcpalm.com/news/2008/may/20/crime-can-strike-fast-
south-florida-malls/

Halbert, S. (1958). The Suspension of the Writ of Habeas Corpus by
President Lincoln. *The American Journal of Legal History, 2*(2).

Hammer, D. (2010, October 25). Full-body scanners are demonstrated at
Louis Armstrong Airport. *Times-Picayune* Retrieved October 31,
2010, from http://www.nola.com/politics/index.ssf/2010/10/full-
body_scanners_demonstrate.html

Handy, S. (2010, October 28). New intrusive TSA pat-down or rub-down?
ABC - KFSN Retrieved October 31, 2010, from http://abclocal.go.
com/kfsn/story?section=news/national_world&id=7753020

Harper, J. (2007). Understanding the Realities of Real ID. *Vital Speeches
of the Day, 73*(5), 208-212.

HB 361 - Prohibits the Department of Revenue from amending its driver's
license application procedures in order to comply with the federal
REAL ID Act. (2009). *Missouri State Legislature* Retrieved October
25, 2010, from http://www.senate.mo.gov/09info/bts_web/Bill.aspx?
SessionType=R&BillID=1894200

HB 1716. (2008, October 15). *MIssouri House of Representatives*
Retrieved December 24, 2008, from http://www.house.mo.gov/
billtracking/bills081/bills/HB1716.HTM

Healey, J. (2008, January 22). The false promise of Real ID. *Los Angeles
Times* Retrieved December 20, 2008, from http://www.latimes.com/
news/opinion/la-oew-healey22jan22,0,5551102.story?coll=la-
opinion-center

Helft, M. (2008, November 11). Google Uses Searches to Track Flu's
Spread. *New York Times* Retrieved January 1, 2009, from
http://www.nytimes.com/2008/11/12/technology/internet/
12flu.html

Hellums, S. (2002). Bits and Bytes: The Carnivore Initiative and the Search and Seizure of Electronic Mail. *William & Mary Bill of Rights Journal, 10*(April).

Herman, E. S., & Chomsky, N. (1988). *Manufacturing consent: The political economy of the mass media.* New york: Pantheon.

Heyman, D., & Carafano, J. J., Ph.D. (2008). *Homeland Security 3.0: Building a National Enterprise to Keep America Free, Safe and Prosperous*: Center for Strategic & International Studies. (C. f. S. I. Studies o. Document Number)

Hoffman, B. (1998). *Inside Terrorism.* London: Victor Gollancz, Ltd.

Holguin, R. (2010, October 29). TSA starts new pat-down screening method. *KABC News* Retrieved October 30, 2010, from http://abclocal.go.com/kabc/story?section=news/national_world&id= 7753461

Hope, C. (2008, October 21). Centuries of British Freedoms being 'broken' by security state, says Sir Ken Macdonald. *Telegraph*, from http://www.telegraph.co.uk/news/newstopics/politics/lawandorder/32 30452/Centuries-of-British-freedoms-being-broken-by-security-state-says-Sir-Ken-Macdonald.html

House Bill No. 1716. (2008, April 8). *Missouri 94th General Assembly* Retrieved April 24, 2008, from http://www.house.mo.gov/ billtracking/bills081/biltxt/perf/HB1716P.htm

HR 2677 - 482R - I Ver. (n.d.). *Arizona State Legislature* Retrieved October 25, 2010, from http://www.azleg.gov/legtext/48leg/2r/bills/ hb2677p.htm

Hsu, S. (2007a, October 27). FEMA Official Apologizes for Staged Briefing With Fake Reporters. *Washington Post* Retrieved January 12, 2009, from http://www.washingtonpost.com/wp-dyn/content/article/2007/10/26/AR2007102602157.html

Hsu, S. (2007b, November 4). Homeland Security Retreats from Facets of 'Real ID'. *Washington Post* Regional. Retrieved February 24, 2009, from http://www.washingtonpost.com/wp-dyn/content/article/2007/ 11/03/AR2007110300890.html

Hubbard, B. (2008, August 13). Police Turn to Secret Weapon: GPS Device. *Washington Post* Retrieved January 8, 2009, from http://www.washingtonpost.com/wp-dyn/content/article/2008/08/12/ AR2008081203275.html?hpid=topnews

Hudson, A. (2007, February 14). Chertoff defends Real ID mandate; Changes sought in visa waivers. *Washington Times* Retrieved February 21, 2009, from http://www.washingtontimes.com /news/2007/feb/13/20070213-111641-9285r/

If you have nothing to hide... (2008, February 14). *Chronicles of Dissent* Retrieved January 11, 2009, from http://www.pogowasright.org /blogs/dissent/?p=828

Image of bombers' deadly journey (2005, July 17). *BBC News* Retrieved January 1, 2009, from http://news.bbc.co.uk/2/hi/uk_news/politics/ 4689739.stm#

Information about Chicago Card and Transit Card. (n.d.). *Chicago Transit Authority* Retrieved October 16, 2010, from http://www. transitchicago.com/travel_information/fares/faremedia.aspx

Intelligence Reform and Terrorism Prevention Act of 2004, 108-458 (2004).

Intelligent Transportation Systems (ITS). (2005, March 18). *United We Ride* Retrieved January 7, 2009, from http://www.unitedweride. gov/MMS-ITS-3-18-05.doc

Intermec to support first RFID standard for tire tracking and traceability. (Technology Trends). (2002, April 1). *Transport Technology Today*, from http://www.allbusiness.com/operations/facilities-office-equipment/181020-1.html

Internet and Computer Monitoring Software. (n.d.). *Workexaminer* Retrieved January 9, 2009, from http://www.workexaminer.com/

Jackson, D. (1999). Protection Of Privacy In The Search And Seizure Of E-Mail: Is the United States Doomed to an Orwellian Future? *Temple Environmental Law & Technology, 17*(Spring).

Jenkins, B. (1986). Defense Against Terrorism. *Political Science Quarterly, 101*(5), 773-786.

Johnson, C. (1958). The Status of Freedom of Expression under the Smith Act. *The Western Political Quarterly, 11*(3).

Johnson, C. (2008, October 4). Guidelines Expand FBI's Surveillance Powers. *Washington Post* Retrieved February 25, 2009, from http://www.washingtonpost.com/wp-dyn/content/article/2008/10/03/ AR2008100303501.htm

Johnston, D. (2003, September 9). Two Years Later: 9/11 Tactics; Official Says Qaeda Recruited Saudi Hijackers to Strain Ties. *The New York Times* Retrieved February 25, 2009, from http://query.nytimes.com/gst/fullpage.html?res=9803E4DD14BF93AA3575AC0A9659C8B63

Jonas, J., & Harper, J. (2006, December 11). Effective Counterterrorism and the Limited Role of Predictive Data Mining. Retrieved February 25, 2009, from http://www.cato.org/pubs/pas/pa584.pdf

Jones, K. C. (2007a, January 22). Thieves Busted By GPS-Enabled Booty *Information Week* Retrieved February 25, 2009, from http://www.informationweek.com/story/showArticle.jhtml?articleID=196902643

Jones, K. C. (2007b, August 21). Vermont Volunteers for Secure ID. *Information Week* Retrieved February 25, 2009, from http://www.informationweek.com/news/internet/showArticle.jhtml?articleID=201801569&cid=RSSfeed_TechWeb

Jones, K. C. (2007, June 1). Web Security Breach Lets Cat Out of Baghdad Embassy Plans. *Information Week* Retrieved June 5, 2007, from http://www.informationweek.com/shared/printableArticle.jhtml?199900280

Jones, K. C. (2008, March 21). Obama, Cliinton, McCain Passport Breaches Expose Human, Not Tech Weakness. *Information Week* Retrieved December 26, 2008, from http://www.informationweek.com/news/management/showArticle.jhtml?articleID=206905232

Jones, S. (1992). Was There a Hawthorne Effect? *The American Journal of Sociology, 98*(3), 451-468.

Jordan, L. J. (2007, March 10). Gonzales, Mueller Admit FBI Broke Law. *Washington Post* Retrieved October 29, 2007, from http://www.washingtonpost.com/wp-dyn/content/article/2007/03/10/AR2007031000324_pf.html

Jose Padilla. (n. d.). *New York Times* Retrieved February 22, 2009, from http://topics.nytimes.com/top/reference/timestopics/people/p/jose_padilla/index.html?inline=nyt-per

Keeping Secrets In Cyberspace: Establishing Fourth Amendment Protection For Internet Communication. (1997). *Harvard Law Review, 110*(May).

Keizer, G. (2007, July 30). Black Hat-bound researcher denied entry into U.S. *Computer World* Retrieved January 10, 2009, from

http://www.computerworld.com/action/article.do?command=viewArt
icleBasic&articleId=9028378&intsrc=news_ts_head

Kerr, D. (2007). *Remarks and Q&A by the Principal Deputy Director of National Intelligence.* Paper presented at the 2007 GEOINT Symposium, San Antonio, TX.

Kerr, J. (2007, April 4). Tire pressure monitoring systems. *Canadian Driver* Retrieved January 8, 2009, from http://www.canadiandriver.com/articles/jk/070404.htm

KFC. (2009, October 30). How Terahertz Waves Tear Apart DNA. *Technology Review (MIT)* Retrieved October 30, 2010, from http://www.technologyreview.com/blog/arxiv/24331/

Klein, N. (2007). *Shock Doctrine, The: The Rise of Disaster Capitalism.* New York: Picador.

Klein, N. (2008, May 29). China's All-Seeing Eye. *Rolling Stone* Retrieved December 30, 2008, from http://www.rollingstone.com/politics/story/20797485/chinas_allseeing_eye

Knickmeyer, E. (2008, October 18). Al-Qaeda Web Forums Abruptly Taken Offline. *Washington Post* Retrieved December 31, 2008, from http://www.washingtonpost.com/wp-dyn/content/article/2008/10/17/AR2008101703367.html

Kravitz, D. (2010, October 29). Dulles last of D.C.-area airports to install full-body scanners. *Washington Post* Retrieved October 30, 2010, from http://www.washingtonpost.com/wp-dyn/content/article/2010/10/29/AR2010102906660.html?hpid=topnews

Krebs, B. (2007, July 6). Three Worked the Web to Help Terrorists. *Washington Post* Retrieved July 10, 2007, from http://www.washingtonpost.com/wp-dyn/content/article/2007/07/05/AR2007070501945_pf.html

Kronholz, J. (2003, October 28, 2003). Reader Beware: Patriot Act Riles an Unlikely Group: Nations Librarians; Fears About Terrorism Clash With Principles of Privacy as Online Searches Surge; FBI: 'Bad Guys' Use Web, Too. *The Wall Street Journal,*

Kuhn, M. (2007). *Federal Dataveillance: Implications for Constitutional Privacy Protections.* New York: LFB Scholarly.

Laqueur, W. (1999). *The New Terrorism: Fanaticism and the Arms of Mass Destruction.* New York: Oxford University Press.

Lawless, M. (2007). The Third Party Doctrine Redux: Internet Search Records and the Case for a "Crazy Quilt" of Fourth Amendment Protection. *UCLA Journal of Law and Technology, 2007*(Spring).

Leckrone, S. E. (1997, March 17, 1997). Turning Back the Clock: The Unfunded Mandates Reform Act of 1995 and Its Effective Repeal of Environmental Legislation. Retrieved August 3, 2008, from http://law.indiana.edu/ilj/oldsite/volumes/v72/no2/leckrone.html

Lenzer, J. (2006, January 14). Doctors outraged at Patriot Act's potential to seize medical records *British Medical Journal* Retrieved January 10, 2009, from http://www.bmj.com/cgi/content/extract/332/7533/69

Levey, S. (2006, July 11). Testimony of Stuart Levey, Under Secretary , Terrorism and Financial Intelligence Before the House Financial Services Subcommittee on Oversight and Investigations. Retrieved November 23, 2008, from http://www.treas.gov/press/releases/hp05.htm

Levy, R. (2003, August 11). Jose Padilla: No Charges and No Trial, Just Jail. *Chicago SunTimes* Retrieved February 22, 2009, from http://www.cato.org/pub_display.php?pub_id=3208

Lewis, C. (2000). The Terror that Failed: Aftermath of the Bombing in Oklahoma City. *Public Administration Review, 60*(3), 201-210.

Limbaugh v. Florida (Fourth District Court of Appeal 2004).

Lincecum, G. (2003). Electronic Surveillance: Protecting the Privacy Ecosystem from the Federal Bureau of Investigation's Carnivore. *Oklahoma City Law Review, 28*(Spring).

Lipowicz, A. (2007, September 13). Testimony: Clock ticking on Real ID compliance. *Washington Technology* Retrieved December 20, 2008, from http://www.washingtontechnology.com/online/1_1/31408-1.html

Liptak, A. (2007, August 13). A Case So Shielded One Side Is in the Dark *New York Times* Retrieved January 10, 2009, from http://select.nytimes.com/2007/08/13/us/13bar.html?_r=1&scp=1&sq=case%20so%20dark%20one%20side%20is%20in%20the%20dark&st=cse

Lofgren, C. (2005, October 11). Hardships of War. *Claremont Institute* Retrieved January 11, 2009, from http://www.claremont.org/publications/crb/id.1082/article_detail.asp

Loyalty & Stored Value Cards. (2004). *CardLogix* Retrieved January 9, 2009, from http://www.cardlogix.com/pdf/LoyaltyAndStoredValue Cards.pdf

MacManus, S. (1991). "Mad" about Mandates: The Issue of Who Should Pay for What Resurfaces in the 1990s. *Publius, 21*(3), 59-75.

Madigan, N. (2008, July 18). Spying uncovered. *Baltimore Sun* Retrieved February 20, 2009, from http://www.baltimoresun.com/ news/local/bal-te.md.spy18jul18,0,3787307.story

Marek, A. (2007, February 11). Escaping the Watch List. *U.S. News and World Report* Retrieved January 11, 2009, from http://www.usnews. com/usnews/news/articles/070211/19watch_print.htm

Margolick, D. (1982, June 4). Reprise on McCarran Act. *The New York Times* Late City Final. Retrieved March 2, 2009, from http://www2.lib.purdue.edu:2118/pqdweb?index=1&did=121563603 &SrchMode=1&sid=2&Fmt=10&VInst=PROD&VType=PQD&RQ T=309&VName=HNP&TS=1236003332&clientId=31343

McCullagh, D. (2010, August 4). Feds admit storing checkpoint body scan images. *CNet News* Retrieved October 30, 2010, from http://news.cnet.com/8301-31921_3-20012583-281.html? part=rss&subj=news&tag=2547-1_3-0-20

McTigue, D. (1999). Marginalizing Individual Privacy on the Internet *Boston University Journal of Science and Technology Law, 5*(Spring).

McWhirter, D., & Bible, J. (1992). *Privacy as a Constitutional Right.* New york: Quorum Books.

MD5 Weakness Allows Fake SSL Certificates To Be Created. (2008, December 30). *SSL Shopper* Retrieved February 22, 2009, from http://www.sslshopper.com/article-md5-weakness-allows-fake-ssl-certificates-to-be-created.html

METRO Group moves closer to its "Future Store" vision with smart merchandising enabled by RFID. (2008, December 23). *IBM* Retrieved January 11, 2009, from http://www-01.ibm.com/ software/success/cssdb.nsf/CS/JSTS-7MLKHS?OpenDocument& Site=software&cty=en_us

Metro opens high-tech shop and Claudia approves. (2003, April 28). *IBM* Retrieved January 11, 2009, from http://web.archive.org/web/

20040228234802/http://www-1.ibm.com/industries/wireless/doc/content/news/pressrelease/872672104.html

Metz, C. (2008). Yahoo! mocks Google Privacy Theatre. *theRegister.com* Retrieved December 23, 2008, from http://www.theregister.co.uk/2008/12/17/yahoo_anonymization_explained/

Milberg, S., Burke, S., Smith, H., & Kallman, E. (1995). Values, Personal Information, Privacy and Regulatory Approaches. *Communications of the ACM, 38*(12).

Milcent, G., & Cai, Y. (2006). Object Detection and Tracking. *ambient intelligence lab* Retrieved January 1, 2009, from http://www.cmu.edu/vis/project5.html

Milgram, S. (1967). Small-World Problem. *Psychology Today, 1*(1), 61-67.

Milgram, S. (1974). *Obedience to Authority: An Experimental View*. New York: Perrenial Classics.

Military Commissions Act of 2006. (2006). *Washington Post* Retrieved February 22, 2009, from http://www.washingtonpost.com/wp-srv/politics/documents/cheney/military_commissions_act.pdf

Million Dollar Netflix. (2006, October 2). *Kiosk.net* Retrieved January 7, 2009, from http://kiosk.net/2006/10/million-dollar-netflix/

Mills, E. (2008, August 6). Hacking electronic-toll systems. *CNET News* Retrieved January 7, 2009, from http://news.cnet.com/8301-1009_3-10009353-83.html

Minimum Standards for Driver's Licenses and Identification Cards Acceptable by Federal Agencies for Official Purposes; Final Rule. (2008). Retrieved. from http://edocket.access.gpo.gov/2008/08-140.htm.

Missing Persons Investigative Best Practices Protocol Unidentified Deceased Persons Investigative Guidelines. (2008, October 30). *New Jersey State Police* Retrieved January 9, 2009, from http://www.njsp.org/divorg/invest/pdf/mpi-best-practices-protocol-103008.pdf

Morris, S. (2010, November 2). New speed camera can catch drivers committing five offences at once. *Guardian UK* Retrieved November 4, 2010, from http://www.guardian.co.uk/world/2010/nov/02/speed-camera-five-offences

Mousseau, M. (2002/2003). Market Civilization and its Clash with Terror. *International Security, 27*(3), 5-29.

Murphy, K. (2007, October 19). Britain's Long Lens of the Law. *Los Angeles Times* Retrieved February 25, 2009, from http://articles.latimes.com/2007/oct/19/world/fg-bigbrother19

Myers, L., Pasternak, D., & Gardella, R. (2005, December 14). Is the Pentagon spying on Americans? *MSNBC* Retrieved February 7, 2009, from http://www.msnbc.msn.com/id/10454316/

Myth Buster: TSA's Watch List is More Than One Million People Strong. (n.d.). *TSA* Retrieved October 31, 2010, from http://www.tsa.gov/approach/mythbusters/tsa_watch_list.shtm

Nakashima, E. (2007, December 22). FBI Prepares Vast Database Of Biometrics. *Washington Post.* Retrieved October 26, 2008, from http://www.washingtonpost.com/wp-dyn/content/article/2007/12/21/AR2007122102544_pf.html

Nakashima, E. (2008a, January 26). Bush Order Expands Network Monitoring. *WashingtonPost.com* Retrieved January 7, 2009, from http://www. washingtonpost.com/wp-dyn/content/article/2008/01/25/AR2008012503261.html?wpisrc=rss_technology

Nakashima, E. (2008b, August 20). Citizens' U.S. Border Crossings Tracked. *Washington Post* Retrieved October 23, 2010, from http://www.washingtonpost.com/wp-dyn/content/article/2008/08/19/AR2008081902811.html?hpid=topnews

Napolitano, A. (2004, March 5). Repeal the Patriot Act. *Wall Street Journal*, p. 14.

National ID and the REAL ID Act. (2010). *Electronic Privacy Information Center* Retrieved October 25, 2010, from http://epic.org/privacy/id-cards/

National Strategy for Combating Terrorism. (2006). Washington, D.C.o. Document Number)

Newmarker, C. (2007, August 10). E-ZPass records out cheater in divorce court. *msnbc* Retrieved January 6, 2009, from http://www. msnbc.msn.com/id/20216302/

Nobles, J. (2000). *State Mandates on Local Governments.* St. Paul, MN: State of Minnesota. (O. o. t. L. Auditor o. Document Number)

Notice of Proposed Rulemaking: Minimum Standards for Driver's Licenses and Identification Cards Acceptable by Federal Agencies for Official Purposes. (2007). Retrieved December 21, 2008, from http:// edocket.access.gpo.gov/2007/07-1009.htm

O'Harrow, R. (1998, March 8). Are Data Firms Getting Too Personal. *Washington Post*. Retrieved November 6, 2008, from http://www. washingtonpost.com/wp-srv/frompost/march98/privacy8.htm

O'Harrow, R. (2005). *No Place To Hide*. New York: Simon & Schuster, Inc.

O'Neill, S. (2008, October 29). Is the TSA violating your privacy with its new body scanning machines? *Budget Travel/Newsweek* Retrieved October 30, 2010, from http://current.newsweek.com/budgettravel/ 2008/10/is_the_tsa_violating_your_priv.html

Officer Suspended For Mailing 'Homewrecker' Flyers. (2008, February 8). *WSB-TV* Retrieved January 11, 2009, from http://www.wsbtv.com/ news/15256835/detail.html

Official 9/11 Death Toll Climbs By One. (2008, October 4). from http://www.cbsnews.com/stories/2008/07/10/national/main4250100.s html

Order Pertaining to Al-Haramain Islamic Foundation et al v Bush et al (C 07-0109 VRW). (2009, January 5). *United States District Court for the Northern District of California* Retrieved January 10, 2009, from http://www.eff.org/files/filenode/att/alharamainorder10509.pdf

Orwell, G. (1961). *1984*. New York: New American Library.

Overview of Enhanced Driver's Licenses. (n.d.). *DHS* Retrieved October 23, 2010, from http://www.cbp.gov/linkhandler/cgov/travel/vacation/ enhanced_dl_fs.ctt/enhanced_dl_fs.pdf

Ozzy Osbourne, The Roots, Cat Stevens: the music at the Rally to Restore Sanity. (2010, November 1). *Baltimore Sun* Retrieved November 5, 2010, from http://weblogs.baltimoresun.com/entertainment/ midnight_sun/blog/2010/11/ozzy_osbourne_the_roots_cat_st.html

Pabst, G. (2006, March 20). Activist gives her voice to immigrant causes *Milwaukee Journal Sentinel*. Retrieved September 28, 2008, from http://www.jsonline.com/story/index.aspx?id=409416

Parent, W. A. (1983). Privacy, Morality and the Law. In J. Feinberg & H. Gross (Eds.), *Philosophy of Law*. Belmont, CA: Wadsworth Publishing Company.

Parking Ticket Management Solutions. (2008, August 19). *Complus Data Innovations, Inc.* Retrieved January 6, 2009, from http://www. complusdata.com/news.asp

Personal Identification - AAMVA International Specification - DL/ID Card Design. (2005). *American Association of Motor Vehicle Administrators* Retrieved December 27, 2008, from http://www. aamva.org/AAMVA/DocumentDisplay.aspx?id={66260AD6-64B9-45E9-A253-B8AA32241BE0}

Phillips, D. (2005). Texas 9-1-1: Emergency telecommunications and the genesis of surveillance infrastructure. *Telecommunications Policy, 29*(11), 843-856.

Phishing Explained. (n.d.). *APACS - the U.K. payments association* Retrieved January 11, 2009, from http://www.banksafeonline.org.uk/ phishing_explained.html

Pincus, W. (2009, November 1). 1,600 are suggested daily for FBI's list. *Washington Post* Retrieved November 24, 2010, from http://www. washingtonpost.com/wp-dyn/content/article/2009/10/31/ AR2009103102141.html

Posner, R. (2006). *Not a Suicide Pact*. New York: Oxford University Press.

Poulsen, K. (2007, August 15). NSA Judge: 'I feel like I'm in Alice in Wonderland'. *Wired.com* Retrieved January 10, 2009, from http://blog.wired.com/27bstroke6/2007/08/nsa-hearing-ope.html

Prevent and Disrupt Terrorist Attacks. (2007). *White House* Retrieved December 28, 2008, from http://www.whitehouse.gov/infocus/ homeland/nshs/2007/sectionV.html

Prince, R. (2008, October 16). Jacqui Smith plans broad new 'Big Brother' surveillance powers *The Telegraph* Retrieved February 20, 2009, from http://www.telegraph.co.uk/news/newstopics/politics/ 3202766/Jacqui-Smith-plans-broad-new-Big-Brother-surveillance-powers.html

Procurement Specification for Whole Body Imager Devices for Checkpoint Operations. (2008, September 23). *TSA* Retrieved October 30, 2010, from http://epic.org/open_gov/foia/TSA_ Procurement_Specs.pdf

Proposed 'Enhanced' Licenses Are Costly to Security and Privacy. (2007, September). *EPIC* Retrieved January 11, 2009, from http://epic.org/ privacy/surveillance/spotlight/0907/default.html

Pulliam, D. (2007, July 9). Employee tried to mask extent of latest VA data breach. *Government Executive* Retrieved November 5, 2010, from http://www.govexec.com/dailyfed/0707/070907p1.htm

Pumphrey, G. (2003, June 19). Types of Terrorism and 9/11. Retrieved September 28, 2008, from http://www.globalresearch.ca/ articles/PUM306A.html

Radil, A. (1999). Document 1: The Right to be Left Alone. *The Surveillance Society* Retrieved November 11, 2008, from http://news.minnesota.publicradio.org/features/199911/15_newsroom _privacy/leftalone.html

Ragan, F. (1971). Justice Oliver Wendell Holmes, Jr., Zechariah Chafee Jr., and the Clear and Present Danger Test for Free Speech: The First Year, 1919. *The Journal of American History, 58*(1).

Rao, V. R., & Tripati, R. (2008, November). Personal Information Integration in e-Government. *eGov* Retrieved January 9, 2009

Real ID Act of 2005, (2005).

Reno, J. (1995). *Procedure for Contacts between the FBI and the Criminal Division Concerning Foreign Intelligence and Foreign Counterintelligence Investigations.* Washington, D.C.: U.S. Depatment of Justiceo. Document Number)

Report From the Field: The USA PATRIOT Act at Work. (2004). U.S. Department of Justiceo. Document Number)

Report into the London Terrorist Attacks on 7 July 2005. (2006). Intelligence and Security Committeeo. Document Number)

Report to the Attorney General and Director of Central Intelligence. (1995). o. Document Number)

Reutty, M. (2007). What Happened to me When the Police Came Knocking. *Computers in Libraries, 27*(6), 10-15.

RFID, A Vision of the Future. (2007). *RSA Laboratories* Retrieved
January 11, 2009, from http://www.rsa.com/rsalabs/node.asp?id=
2117

Risen, J., & Lichtblau, E. (2005, December 15). Bush Lets U.S. Spy on
Callers Without Courts. *New York Times* Retrieved January 9, 2009,
from http://www.nytimes.com/2005/12/16/politics/16program.html

Rotenberg, M. (2006). Real ID, Real Trouble. *Commnucations of the
ACM, 49*(3), 128.

Rules and Regulations / Vol.74, No. 247 / 68478. (2009). *Federal Register*
Retrieved October 31, 2010, from http://frwebgate.access.gpo.
gov/cgi-bin/getpage.cgi?dbname=2009_register&page=68478&
position=all

Rumsfeld, D. (2001, September 24). DoD News Briefing - Secretaries
Rumsfeld and Martinez. Retrieved November 17, 2008, from
http://www.defenselink.mil/transcripts/transcript.aspx?transcriptid=1
927

S. 717 [110th]: Identification Security Enhancement Act of 2007 (2008).
GovTrack Retrieved October 25, 2010, from http://www.
govtrack.us/congress/bill.xpd?bill=s110-717

Savage, C. (2008). President weakens espionage oversight. *Boston Globe
Online* Retrieved December 31, 2008, from http://www.boston.com/
news/nation/articles/2008/03/14/president_weakens_espionage_overs
ight/

Savage, N. (2010, March). X-ray Body Scanners Arriving at Airports.
IEEE Spectrum Retrieved October 31, 2010, from http://spectrum.
ieee.org/biomedical/imaging/xray-body-scanners-arriving-at-airports

Scheck, T. (2006). Hatch wants end to selling of driver's license info.
Minnesota Public Radio Retrieved January 9, 2009, from http://
news.minnesota.publicradio.org/features/2006/01/04_scheckt_id/

Schneider, J., & Schneider, P. (2002). The Mafia and al-Qaeda: Violent
and Secretive Organizations in Comparative and Historical
Perspective. *American Anthropologist, 104*(3), 776-782.

Schneier, B. (2006, May 18). The Eternal Value of Privacy. Retrieved
December 10, 2008, from http://www.wired.com/news/
columns/1,70886-0.html

Schneier, B. (2007a, January 25). In Praise of Security Theater. *Wired.com* Retrieved January 2, 2009, from http://www.wired.com/print/politics/ security/commentary/securitymatters/2007/01/72561

Schneier, B. (2007b, May 8). Testimony of Bruce Schneier *United States Senate Committee on the Judiciary* Retrieved February 20, 2009, from http://judiciary.senate.gov/hearings/testimony.cfm?id=2746& wit_id=6454

Schweitzer, B. (2008, January 18). Letter to Governor Ritter. *Wired.com* Retrieved November 22, 2010, from http://www.wired.com/images_ blogs/threatlevel/files/real_id_to_gov_ritter_011808_pdf1.pdf

Scowcroft, B. (2002, September 5). Speech: Remarks by Brent Scowcroft at the U.S. Institute of Peace Conference on America's Challenges in a Changed World. Retrieved November 17, 2008, from http://www. ffip.com/interviews090502.htm

Secretary Janet Napolitano. (2009, July 20). *Department of Homeland Security* Retrieved October 27, 2010, from http://www.dhs.gov/ xabout/structure/bio_1231864742617.shtm

Senate Committee Substitute for House Concurrent Resolution No. 20 - 1878S.04C. (2007, June 7). *Missouri Legislature* Retrieved October 25, 2010, from http://epic.org/privacy/id-cards/mo_hcr20.pdf

Sharkey, J. (2006, February 14). Jumping Through Hoops to Get Off the No-Fly List *New York Times* Retrieved November 1, 2010, from http://www.nytimes.com/2006/02/14/business/14road.html?_r=1

Sharkey, J. (2010, November 2). Opt Out of a Body Scan? Then Brace Yourself. *New York Times* Retrieved November 3, 2010, from http://finance.yahoo.com/news/Opt-Out-of-a-Body-Scan-Then-nytimes-3016411705.html?x=0

Significant Terrorist Incidents, 1961-2003: A Brief Chronology. (2004). Retrieved September 27, 2008, from http://www.state.gov/ r/pa/ho/pubs/fs/5902.htm

Sim card data recovery Software. (n.d.). *datadoctor.org* Retrieved January 8, 2009, from http://www.datadoctor.org/partition-recovery/sim-card.html

Singel, R. (2007, June 12). AT&T 'Spy Room' Documents Released, Confirm Wired News' Earlier Publication. *Wired* Retrieved February 22, 2009, from http://blog.wired.com/27bstroke6/2007/06/ att_spy_room_do.html

Singel, R. (2008a, January 18). Montana Governor Foments Real ID Rebellion. *Wired.com* Retrieved December 25, 2008, from http://blog.wired.com/27bstroke6/2008/01/montana-governo.html

Singel, R. (2008b, March 21). Montana Governor: DHS 'Blinks' on Real ID. *Wired* Retrieved February 25, 2009, from http://blog.wired.com/27bstroke6/2008/03/montana-gov-dhs.html

Singel, R. (2009, March 17). Australia Censors Wikileaks Page. *Wired* Retrieved November 2, 2010, from http://www.wired.com/threatlevel/2009/03/australia-censo/

Sisk, R. (2010). Graphic full body scanners headed to JFK and LaGuardia, eventually. *NY Daily News* Retrieved October 30, 2010, from http://www.nydailynews.com/ny_local/2010/10/19/2010-10-19_body_scanners_at_jfk__laguardia_to_show_graphic_images_so_opt_for_a_patdown_or_w.html

Slobogin, C. (2007). *Privacy at Risk: The New Government Surveillance and the Fourth Amendment.* Chicago: The University of Chicago Press.

SmarTrip Questions & Answers. (n.d.). *WMATA* Retrieved October 17, 2010, from http://www.wmata.com/fares/smartrip/smartrip_qanda.cfm#balance_protected

Smelser, M. (1954). George Washington and the Alien and Sedition Acts. *The American Historical Review, 59*(2), 322-334.

Solomon, D. (2006, October 15). For God and Country. *New York Times Magazine,* 22.

Solomon, J. (2007, June 14). FBI Finds It Frequently Overstepped in Collecting Data. *Washington Post,* p. 1. Retrieved June 20, 2007, from http://www.washingtonpost.com/wp-dyn/content/article/2007/06/13/AR2007061302453_pf.html

Solove, D. (2006). *A Brief History of Information Privacy Law*: George Washington University Law School. (G. W. U. L. School o. Document Number)

Songini, M. (2006, June 12). Wisconsin law bars forced RFID implants. *Computerworld* Retrieved February 21, 2009, from http://www.computerworld.com/action/article.do?command=viewArticleBasic&articleId=111542

Songini, M. (2007, April 12). N.D. bans forced RFID chipping. *Computerworld* Retrieved February 21, 2009, from http://www.computerworld.com/action/article.do?command=viewArt icleBasic&articleId=9016385

Spafford, E. (2006, December 18). Quotable Spaf. *Gene Spafford's Personal Pages* Retrieved January 2, 2009, from http://homes.cerias.purdue.edu/~spaf/quotes.html

Spafford, E. (2008, September 3). Security Through Obscurity. *CERIAS* Retrieved February 21, 2009, from http://www.cerias.purdue.edu/ site/blog/post/security_through_obscurity/

Spellman, J. (2008, April 28). Behind the Scenes: New airport scanner reveals all. *CNN* Retrieved October 31, 2010, from http://articles.cnn.com/2008-04-28/travel/body.scanner_1_tsa-official-image-tube?_s=PM:TRAVEL

Spinetto, N. (2008, February 7). Deputy fired. *WINK-TV News* Retrieved January 11, 2009, from http://www.winknews.com/news/local/ 15408931.html

Standards - U.S. License Technology. (2008). *American Association of Motor Vehicle Administrators* Retrieved December 27, 2008, from http://aaa.aamva.org/knowledgecenter/standards/ uslicensetechnology.htm

States Challenge Homeland Security's ID Deadline [Electronic. (2008). Version]. *Atipshop*. Retrieved March 30, from http://atipshop.com/ index.php?option=com_content&task=view&id=21&Itemid=1

Stobart, J., & Rotella, S. (2008, August 2). Jury fails to reach verdict in London attacks. *Seattle Times* Retrieved January 1, 2009, from http://seattletimes.nwsource.com/html/nationworld/2008087486_lond on02.html

Stone, G. (2003). Civil Liberties in Wartime. *Journal of Supreme Court History, 28*(3).

Strickland, L. S., & Hunt, L. E. (2005). Technology, security, and individual privacy: New tools, new threats, and new public perceptions. *Journal of the American Society for Information Science and Technology, 56*(3).

Strub, H. (1989). The Theory of Panoptical Control: Bentham's Panopticon and Orwell's Nineteen Eighty Four. *The Journal of Behavioral Sciences, 25*, 40-59.

Student Pranked by Philadelphia Airport TSA Worker. (2010, January 25).
    ABC News Retrieved October 31, 2010, from http://abcnews.go.
    com/Travel/wireStory?id=9655227

Sullivan, B. (2006, October 19). 'La difference' is stark in EU, U.S.
    privacy laws. *MSNBC* Retrieved January 10, 2009, from
    http://www.msnbc.msn.com/id/15221111/

Sullivan, E. (2010, October 28). TSA rolling out new pat-down technique
    at airports. *Washington Post* Retrieved October 30, 2010, from
    http://www.washingtonpost.com/wp-dyn/content/article/2010/
    10/28/AR2010102807130.html

Svensson, P. (2008, March 24). HD videoconferencing: In your living
    room. *USA Today* Retrieved January 3, 2009, from http://www.
    usatoday.com/tech/products/2008-03-24-hd-videoconferencing-
    home_N.htm

SWIFT to stop processing EU banking data in the US. (2007, October 15).
    The Register.com Retrieved October 17, 2007, from http://www.
    theregister.co.uk/2007/10/15/swift_processing_halt/print.html

Swire, P. (2002). The Surprising Virtues of the New Financial Privacy
    Law. *Minnesota Law Review* Retrieved October 26, 2010, from
    http://www.federalreserve.gov/SECRS/2004/April/20040401/R-
    1173/R-1173_24_1.pdf

Tankersley, J. (2007, November 16). Audit: Terrorists got U.S. aid:
    Agency's screening called inadequate. *Chicago Tribune* Retrieved
    January 11, 2009, from http://archives.chicagotribune.com/
    2007/nov/16/news/chi-terror_aid16nov16

Temple-Rastin, D. (2007a, September 9). Enemy Within? Not Quite.
    Washington Post Retrieved January 11, 2009, from http://www.
    washingtonpost.com/wp-dyn/content/article/2007/09/07/
    AR2007090702049.html

Temple-Rastin, D. (2007b, July 4). In U.S., Calls Grow for U.K.-Style
    Security Cameras *All Things Considered, NPR* Retrieved January 1,
    2009, from http://www.npr.org/templates/story/story.php?storyId=
    11737314

Terrorism, Al Qaeda, and the Muslim World, (2003).

Tilly, C. (2004). Terror, Terrorism, Terrorists. *Sociological Theory, 22*(1),
    5-13.

Top Al Qaeda Leader Abu Ubaida al-Masri Confirmed Dead in Pakistan. (2008, April 9). *Fox News* Retrieved January 1, 2009, from http://www.foxnews.com/story/0,2933,348668,00.html

Tortora, V. R. (1998). The Seventh Sense. *Focus, 45*(1), 15-18.

Townsend, M., & Asthana, A. (2008, March 16). Put young children on DNA list, urge police. *The Guardian* Retrieved February 20, 2009, from http://www.guardian.co.uk/society/2008/mar/16/youthjustice. children

Tran, M. (2010, March 24). Airport worker given police warning for 'misusing' body scanner. *Guardian.co.uk* Retrieved October 31, 2010, from http://www.guardian.co.uk/uk/2010/mar/24/airport-worker-warned-body-scanner

TSA Secure Flight and You. (2009). *TSA* Retrieved October 31, 2010, from www.hhs.gov/travel/tsa_secure_flight_and_you.doc

Tushnet, M. (Ed.). (2008). *I Dissent*. Boston: Beacon Press.

Twelve Senators Urge Frist to Keep Real ID Act Off Supplemental Appropriations Bill Sweeping Proposal Needs Deliberate Consideration. (2005, April 11). Retrieved December 20, 2008, from http://hsgac.senate.gov/public/index.cfm?FuseAction= PressReleases.Print&PressRelease_id=b456811f-b97a-4d4c-8503-cacbaaa649ca&suppresslayouts=true

U.S. automobile registrations. (2001). Retrieved 2008, October 25, from http://vnweb.hwwilsonweb.com/hww/results/results_ single_fulltext.jhtml?_DARGS=/hww/results/results_single.jhtml.14

U.S. Dignitaries Dedicate New American Embassy in Baghdad. (2009, January 5, 2009). *Embassy of the United States: Baghdad, Iraq* Retrieved October 16, 2010, from http://iraq.usembassy.gov/pr-01052009.html

Understanding the Realities of REAL ID: A Review of Efforts to Secure Drivers Licenses and Identification Cards, U. S. Senate (2007).

Uniting and Strengthening America by Providing Appropriate Tools Required to Intercept and Obstruct Terrorism (USA PATRIOT Act) ACT of 2001, (2001).

Vanderhoof, R. (2007). Executive Director's Letter. *Smart Card Talk* Retrieved December 27, 2008, from http://www.smartcardalliance. org/newsletter/march_2007/letter_0307.html

Vermont Issues New Enhanced Driver's License. (2009, January 5). *AAMVA* Retrieved January 11, 2009, from http://www.aamva.org/Publications/TWiR/2009/Month01/Day05/VTEDLID.htm

Vijayan, J. (2008, December 8). GPS tracking of high credit-risk drivers: Good practice or privacy violation? . *ComputerWorld* Retrieved January 8, 2009, from http://blogs.computerworld.com/gps_tracking_privacy_violation

Vlahos, J. (2008, January). Surveillance Society: New High-Tech Cameras Are Watching You. *Popular Mechanics* Retrieved January 6, 2009, from http://www.popularmechanics.com/technology/military_law/4236865.html?page=2

Volokh, A. (1997). n Guilty Men. *University of Pennsylvania Law Review 146.*

Warren, S. (2010, January 5). Full-body airport scanners face further delays over fears they breach child porn laws *Mail Online* Retrieved October 30, 2010, from http://www.dailymail.co.uk/news/article-1240738/Full-body-airport-scanners-create-naked-images-pass-child-pornography-laws.html

Warren, S., & Brandeis, L. (1890). The Right to Privacy. *Harvard Law Review, 4*(5).

Warrior, J., McHenry, E., & McGee, K. (2003). They Know Where You Are. *IEEE Spectrum, 40*(7), 20-25.

Warshak v. United States: Federal Appeals Court Holds Email Constitutionally Protected. (2007, July 24). *Center for Democracy and Technology* Retrieved February 5, 2009, from http://www.cdt.org/security/20070726warshak-analysis.pdf

Washburn, G. (2007, August 12). City rakes in revenue from tickets: Car-related fines plug $210 million hole in budget. *Chicago Tribune* Retrieved January 6, 2009, from http://archives.chicagotribune.com/2007/aug/12/news/chi-carcash_bd_12aug12

Weiss, R. (2007, October 9). Dragonfly or Insect Spy? Scientists at Work on Robobugs. *Washington Post* Retrieved October 17, 2010, from http://www.washingtonpost.com/wp-dyn/content/article/2007/10/08/AR2007100801434.html

Welch, M. (2003). Get Ready for PATRIOT II [Electronic Version]. *AlterNet.* Retrieved November 18, 2007, from http://www.alternet.org/module/printversion/15541

Wettstein, D. (2010, March). New SWIFT architecture proves productive. *ClearIT* Retrieved November 21, 2010, from http://www. telekurs.com/dl_tkicch_clearit43swift.pdf

Which is it: Millimeter Wave or Backscatter? (2008, May 25). *TSA Blog, The* Retrieved October 30, 2010, from http://blog.tsa.gov/2008/05/ which-is-it-millimeter-wave-or.html

WHTI | Western Hemisphere Travel Initiative. (n.d.). Retrieved October 23, 2010, from http://www.getyouhome.gov/html/eng_map.html

Will Real ID Actually Make Us Safer? An Examination of Privacy and Civil Liberties Concerns, United States Senate, 110th Congress, First Sess. 1-247 (2007).

Williams, I. (2007). US state bans forced RFID tagging of humans [Electronic Version]. *vnunet.com*. Retrieved September 12, 2007, from http://www.vnunet.com/articles/print/2197977

Wolf, N. (2007). *The End of America*. White River Junction, VT: Chelsea Green Publishing Company.

Yoo, D. (1996). Review: Captivating Memories: Museology, Concentration Camps, and Japanese American History. *48*(4), 680-699.

Yoo, J. (2006). *War by Other Means*. New York: Atlantic Monthly Press.

Young, P. (2001). The Case Against Carnivore: Preventing Law Enforcement from Devouring Privacy. *Indiana Law Review, 35*.

Zaba, C. (2010, January 4). Body scanners threaten children's rights. *Guardian UK* Retrieved October 30, 2010, from http://www.guardian.co.uk/ commentisfree/libertycentral/2010/jan/04/airport-body-scanners

Zalud, B. (2007, April). Real ID or No Real ID? *Security, 51*.

Zetter, K. (2010, October 7). Caught Spying on Student, FBI Demands GPS Tracker Back. Retrieved November 5, 2010, from http://www.wired.com/threatlevel/2010/10/fbi-tracking-device/all/1

INDEX